"*The Day I Died* is an inspiring story of Carole Petiet's healing journey from a catastrophic skiing accident through the underworld of our often contemptuous and indifferent medical care system, and out the other side to a nearly miraculous recovery. Her story is more than a cold medical chart; it is a heated parable of survival, a passionate demand for patient rights, and a mythic tale of how the broken shell of Humpty-Dumpty was put back together again. In so doing, she reveals to us the vital importance of combining inner psychological work with outer physical therapy, which for her consisted of Chinese medicine, rest, exercise, laughter, time and love. Hers is an inspiring tale because she not only shows she healed her broken body but how she opened her heart again to the joy of life. Your own desire to heal whatever is broken in you will be strengthened by your reading of this book."

Phil Cousineau, author of *The Art of Pilgrimage*, and
Beyond Forgiveness: Reflections on Atonement

"Carole Petiet can write this book because she not only lived through her own deep trauma, but moved through her recovery of that trauma with a great sense of curiosity, exploration, and willingness to share her journey. Her memoir is an engaging and accessible example of utilizing SE™, a powerful approach to healing. This book is filled with generous and transparent gifts to help others in their personal healing journeys."

Kathy Kain, MA, Senior Faculty in the Somatic
Experiencing® training program, author, and provides
workshops via her Somatic Practice Programs

"Thank you for writing this memoir – it demonstrates the power of resilience and of determination and perseverance. …Thanks for writing this book – it will help others."

Douglas Fredrick, MD, Clinical Professor of
Ophthalmology, Stanford University School of Medicine

"*The Day I Died* is an inspiring memoir about recovery from a severe accident and brain injury. Many patients do not want to be 'passive recipients' of health care administered treatments: they want to be listened to, and to be fully involved in all decision-making about their own treatments and their own bodies. With her compelling storytelling, Petiet shows us how to navigate hospitals and rehabilitation, and to skillfully utilize the healing power of Integrative Medicine to find acceptance, peace, and gratitude."

Brenda Townes, PhD, neuropsychologist, Professor
Emeritus, Department of Psychiatry and Behavioral Sciences,
University of Washington School of Medicine

"The Notes and Resources section of *The Day I Died* is a valuable resource that by itself is well worth the cost of Carole's book."

Roger E. Spence, PhD, LCSW

"I loved it. Excellent and compelling reading that chronicles one woman's journey of recovery after traumatic brain injury."

Deborah Doherty, MD, Physical Medicine and Rehabilitation,
Chief Medical Officer for CareMeridian, which provides
subacute residential services to brain injured individuals

"Dr. Carole Petiet has written a moving, powerful story about her own recovery from a severe ski accident that resulted in multiple serious injuries including head trauma and loss of function in her right eye. She describes the crucial elements of her own healing process, including the skill of full inner attunement along with Integrative Medicine, and shows readers how to navigate the labyrinth of western, eastern, and holistic medicine. She also discusses and demonstrates the effectiveness of Somatic Experiencing® along with hypnosis, EMDR, and other alternative methods of healing and pain control. I highly recommend *The Day I Died* to anyone suffering from trauma, their loved ones, and those who treat them, and to any person seeking inspiration in the face of catastrophe."

Maggie Phillips, PhD, psychologist and author of four
books—*Healing the Divided Self; Finding the Energy to Heal:
How EMDR, Hypnosis, TFT, Imagery and Body-Focused
Healing Can Help Restore Mindbody Health; Reversing Chronic
Pain;* and (with Peter Levine) *Freedom From Pain*

The Day I Died

BRAIN TRAUMA AND THE JOURNEY BACK

For Brenda,

Blessings to you in your own life journey,

Carole Petiet, PhD

Carole Petiet

ARCHWAY PUBLISHING

Archway Publishing books may be ordered through booksellers or by contacting:

Archway Publishing
1663 Liberty Drive
Bloomington, IN 47403
www.archwaypublishing.com
1 (888) 242-5904

Author photo by James Garrahan
Ski photo by Roger Laurilla
Cover photo by Carole Petiet

ISBN: 978-1-4808-2843-8 (sc)
ISBN: 978-1-4808-2844-5 (hc)
ISBN: 978-1-4808-2845-2 (e)

Library of Congress Control Number: 2016906710

Print information available on the last page.

Archway Publishing rev. date: 08/12/2016

To Nicole,
for inspiring me to fight so hard for life,
and to Ayala,
for encouraging me to write this book.

Contents

Preface

My mind inches up to the surface, waking, but not to everyday consciousness. I take a breath and open my eye.

Only one eye? What is going on?

I find myself enclosed by metal bars that form a sort of cage around my bed. I am terrified. *Where am I?* I look around frantically, trying to understand.

Straining to see beyond the bars, my vision slowly clears, and I see a calendar that seems far away, on a wall across the room. The calendar is open to May. *But wait, it's April; I'm supposed to be in Paris. It has to be April.*

Everything still looks hazy. There's a hanging TV near a door. *Is this a dream?* I wonder. So I pinch the skin on my forearm. It hurts, and I realize: *This is not a dream. This is for real.*

What is this? What the hell? As I pinch my arm, I see an IV tube. It dawns on me that I must be in a hospital. But, I wonder, *Why is my bed in a zoo cage? What has happened to me? What is going on?*

A nurse walks in. … Before I can form words to speak, I slide back down into sleep. …

I have a glimpse of Nicole[1] arriving with a plate of food. I feel so happy to see her. I reach out. …

I wake up confused. I feel agitated: in tremendous pain all over my body, terrified, angry, upset. I hear jabbering going on around me. Slowly the jabbering begins to take the forms of familiar words, and I hear my name. Then I realize that people are talking about me, about how I'm doing, as if I'm not there. I feel more angry, and I think, *Why don't you ask me*?

The obscuring mental fog continues for days, occasionally broken up by hospital staff or visitors. Mostly, I sleep. I need to sleep. My brain is off line. I desperately need to sleep. And I do sleep, as much as possible, but I am interrupted by the inevitable intrusions of staff and hospital protocol. This agitates me more.

I wake up again, and my friend Margaret[2] is sitting next to me. I feel her hand, hear her voice, and I know she loves me. As I gradually focus on Margaret, I see the broken smile that lines her face. She looks forlorn. Remembering that Margaret is my On Call person during my Paris vacation, I am aware of saying, "What happened to me?"

Margaret bursts into tears, and I try to reassure her: "Don't worry, Sweetheart. I'm going to get well."

In answer, she looks at me with more tears streaming from her eyes and blurts, "I'm afraid you won't. You've asked me what happened many times. I'm afraid you may never get your memory back."

"Oh."

Then Margaret tells me the accident story and how I rose like Lazarus from the dead.

The first inspiration for writing this book came in a moment of pure rage. I was in a hospital for inpatient rehabilitation, not heard or seen for who I really still was by many of the medical personnel, and even by some of my friends and colleagues. I felt powerless and frightened. I was furious about the medical establishment, the state of healthcare in our country. I was angry and hurt about how I was being treated by all but a few. At that point, I wanted to write a book about the wrongs that were done to me under the guise of good healthcare.

But first, I needed to invest my full energy toward healing. My body was exhausted from the trauma.

Then, as I navigated my process of healing beyond trauma, with the help of loving family, friends, and professionals, my focus shifted toward sharing what I learned to help others. I am a nurse, psychologist, and athlete, and these experiences helped me choose how I responded after my accident. That is one of my motivations for writing—to let others know what I learned, in case they run into similar experiences. Also, I believe I was given the gift of survival in part so that I could share with others my experience-based knowledge and understanding about how to recover from severe injury.

Later, the process of writing this book, in itself, became a part of my healing. I hope the perspective that comes from my experience will inspire and empower others.

Foreword

Carole Petiet is a registered nurse, clinical psychologist, and world-class athlete who describes her return to life after it was briefly snuffed out by a harrowing accident. Weaving the complex story of recovery after trauma, Carole also shares a myriad of hard earned personal experiences as well as knowledge gleaned from 40 years of work with people as a helping professional.

This book will resonate with anyone sorting through the downs that inevitably occur in the process of life. Carole focuses on moving across the deep valley to the up side, toward healing, and beyond trauma. Perseverance, patience, vigilance, deep inner attunement, and relationships are key ingredients in these stories.

Carole's experiences are shocking at times, humorous at times, heartfelt, and imbedded with hundreds of tips to inform and empower you. She encourages you not to accept blindly what authority figures may tell you, but to tune into your own body and be more trusting of your instincts. Her stories also challenge our esteemed colleagues in the helping professions, particularly the mental and physical healthcare professions: To stop and reflect on how we are treating people. To consider what we are saying and how our practices are perceived by the people receiving our care. To ask, listen to, see, and respect our patients.

Written by Professor Ayala Malach Pines, PhD[1] (before her untimely death in 2012).

Author's Note

All stories are true, based on memory, numerous conversations with people involved, and medical records. There are no composite stories, and I have chosen not to describe a number of events that are irrelevant to my reasons for writing this book. I have mentioned loved ones, family and friends, by their accurate first names, except for a few whose names have been changed for protection of privacy and identity.

I include some italicized excerpts from personal journals, medical records, opinions and recollections of others, and personal thoughts, most of them preluding each chapter.

For the sake of narrative flow, I have saved valuable information about healers and a number of topics for the Notes and Resources at the end of the book, including: Integrative Medicine for healing, brain plasticity, healing of eyes, treatment of trauma and helping children in the aftermath of trauma, somatic therapy and Somatic Experiencing®, ski safety, humor, and gratitude.

I was watching the races from about one-third of the way down the racecourse and saw a woman when she caught the edge of her ski and went sliding downhill really fast and hard. She disappeared into the well of a tree, and I thought to myself: 'This is not good.' So I raced down there as quickly as I could. There were maybe two or three people there, and I learned that this woman crumpled against the tree was Carole. I could tell it was bad immediately, so I told everyone standing there to call 911 and to ask for a helicopter. I took my skis off, got down, and looked at her. She was completely still. Lifeless essentially. There was so much blood – from the fractures in her skull and also coming out of her every orifice – mouth, ears, nose, and even her eyes, which were fixed and dilated. "Call a helicopter now!" I shouted, in case no one had. I knew that moving her could risk further damage as we are taught to never shift someone with a neck or back injury unless the situation requires life-saving extrication.

She wasn't breathing, and I shook her briefly. Then I realized I was going to have to go mouth to mouth, and I didn't even have time to consider the health risks. I grabbed her jaw, did the jaw-thrust maneuver and at the same time reached in to pull her tongue down and towards me. As I did this, it must have opened up her throat passage, as suddenly she coughed violently and took a deep breath inwards. There was blood everywhere. This breathing action gave her some energy.

As with most major head injuries, there is the natural Fight-or-Fight reaction and adrenaline kicks in. Carole started to violently shake and move, so I got behind her, held her head steady, and said, "Don't move. Don't move!" But she kept thrashing away, so I asked some bystanders who had now gathered to help hold her down. It seemed like a long time until the Ski Patrol arrived. They immediately started to take over, but I protected her neck and said that they HAD to call for a helicopter. Then I told them exactly what had happened and how I found her, as well as explaining that I was a First Responder volunteer fire fighter. Carole was still flailing and trying to fight all of us off, but the Ski Patrol quickly maneuvered a backboard under her, strapped her in, and took her down the slope behind their snowmobile.

A few minutes later, the sound of the air ambulance helicopter clattered, and I honestly thought it would be too late. Surely such a head injury and that much blood obviously settling into her lungs would have been the end of this woman.

(Recollection of accident written by Toby Rowland-Jones[1], the man who saved my life.)

Family Fun Race: The Day I Died

My daughter, Nicole, was a racer with a ski education foundation for children in Northern California. She raced with her team (ages five to ten) in Sierra Nevada Mountain resorts, on weekends and vacations during California ski season. Nicole loves speed, and I was happy to be able to give her this opportunity since I had been too poor to ski when I was very young. Being a natural at skiing, I imagined I might have been a good racer, but I was just an expert free skier.

It was the end of the season for the ski team and a big weekend of celebrations: an awards ceremony, dinner, and silent auction fundraiser on Saturday, and the Family Fun Relay Race on Sunday, April 16, 2000. I skied with Nicole, her friends, and my friends on Saturday. We partied at the fundraiser Saturday evening. Afterward, a group of us spent the night at our cabin in the El Dorado National Forest near Lake Tahoe.

I wanted to go back to Berkeley early Sunday morning, to finish getting ready for our trip to Paris on Monday. It was Nicole's spring vacation, she was in 4th grade, and we were both excited about going back to Paris.

Against my own instincts, I decided to stay in the mountains and join in the Family Fun Relay Race on Sunday. Nicole, her coach Lori, another racer, and I made a relay group of four in the

Orphaned Female Family Team category. We laughed about this race team category, happy to be strong female skiers who wanted to ski together. The order for our relay was quickly decided: "Nicole, why don't you go first, to give us a fast start? Carole, we'd like for you to go last. We hope this will speed us to a first place finish in our category. OK?"

Nicole and I each said, "Sure."

Then Nicole and the other girl on the racing team added, "We really, really want to win this race, and we think we can. We have a great relay team."

Relieved that our plan was easily made, I thought, *I'll give this my best shot. And I'm motivated to ski quickly because I want to get this race over with, go home to Berkeley, finish packing, and be ready to leave for our vacation tomorrow morning.*

There was a lot of joking among the skiers about the racecourse that morning:

"This is really a scary race course."

"Yeah. Steep. Really steep."

"World-class giant slalom terrain. Watch out!"

"Why couldn't they set this up on a more challenging slope?"

The Family Fun Relay Race was on an intermediate run, Mokelumne, and I did not take the simple Giant Slalom course very seriously. It was ho-hum compared to the Monashees, Taos, Jackson Hole, Aspen, Telluride, Squaw Valley, Mammoth, Whistler Blackcomb, and other great ski mountains.

Nicole, the other racer, and Lori—their coach—finessed their way quickly to the finish line. Then it was my turn for the last leg of our relay.

Because of what happened, I have no memory of my race. This sort of amnesia is an expected outcome of traumatic injury, particularly with a head injury. By reports, I was having an excellent race. Thankfully, Toby Rowland-Jones stopped and watched me fly down the racecourse. The relay races were nearly finished, it was warm, the snow was soft, and I caught a ski edge in a deep rut going around the third gate from the finish. I lost my balance, and with the power of speed I swung around and landed flat on my back, head first, and straight into a tree.

Toby was a first responder in the Big Sur area of California Coastal Highway 1, where the many cliffs by the Pacific Ocean make rescue complicated in case of accidents. When I did not start moving immediately after my fall, Toby skied over to assess the situation. The description I share here comes from conversations with Toby and others who were at the accident site, plus medical records.

Toby's description: "You were having a brilliant run, so I stopped to watch. Then you crashed and disappeared in a tree well. When there was no movement, I went straight to where you were: head down, face up. I reckon that I arrived within 90 seconds of your crash into the trees. You were bleeding worse than any car accident victim I've ever seen, even off the cliffs along the Big Sur Coastal Highway. You had no pulse or respiration, and your eyes were fixed and dilated."

As a nurse, I know it takes only five minutes without oxygen to become brain dead. If Toby had waited for the ski patrol to arrive with their gear, I would have been history.

Thank God, Toby arrived with his skill and courage. He directed others to call immediately for a helicopter Flight for Life rescue.

As we discussed my accident months later, Toby realized that he normally would have considered the need for protective gear before doing CPR. But he quickly acted as a skilled first responder, moved in to begin CPR instinctively as he thought, *Oh bugger: she gets help now or never.*

Toby opened my airway with a jaw thrust: pulled my jaw forward and lifted my tongue. Then I coughed up a large amount of clotted blood and woke up. Toby later told me, "It was like you jump started yourself. I didn't even have to do CPR. But I had a hell of a time keeping your airway clear because you were bleeding so badly." Being a nurse, I know that I was on the cusp of death, my heart, lungs, and brain ready to respond only if I could get oxygen. Toby helped me get that life-reviving air.

It was not easy. I was a wild woman in that tree well, by all reports. It took five strong people to hold slender Carole down, to keep me relatively still and safe while Toby worked to keep my airway clear. Toby was assisted by Brian Clark, another medically savvy friend of the racers. They were worried about my head, neck, spinal cord, and back, unclear as to what had been broken or what could get damaged further. This kind of thrashing in a combative and agitated way is classic behavior when an injured person is gasping for air and fighting for life. It can be scary to others, but it is a good instinctive response.

Fifteen minutes after the accident, the professional ski patrol did arrive with gear. They put a cervical collar around my neck, strapped me to a backboard to help protect my spinal cord, and very carefully, with one patroller cradling my head, transported me to the first aid clinic. But if Toby and Brian hadn't stopped to watch me race, and chosen to help, I would have died before the ski patrol reached me. So, in retrospect, it is confusing—even appalling—that no trained first responders were posted at the top of the racecourse by the resort, and that this has not become standard operating procedure for *all* races.

At the clinic, I was manually restrained while two IVs were started, one in each arm, so I could be given strong drugs to sedate me. My ski gear was cut and removed. When sedated enough, I was intubated (a big tube put down my throat to get oxygen more easily to my lungs). I had active arterial bleeding from a large laceration on the right side of my head, which the doctor quickly closed with 20 staples from a medical staple gun. Tubes were then inserted into my stomach and bladder. Every time I started to wake up, I was drugged with Versed, to paralyze and sedate me, so that I would not harm myself in my continued instinctive fight for life. After an X-ray of my neck, I was readied for helicopter transport.

Friends and coaches kept Nicole from me in the tree well ordeal, not wanting to allow a close-up view of my accident to traumatize her further. Nicole only saw me in the tree well from a distance when she was below at the finish line, where she was physically restrained and shrieking to see me in the tree well. To this day, Nicole says, "It still angers me that that choice was taken away from me."

Nicole did later see me up close in the first aid clinic just before my Flight for Life. With bandages and tubes, I was drugged and unable to speak as Nicole, weeping, sputtered, "Goodbye, Mom."

Then the helicopter whisked me away to Washoe Medical Center in Reno, Nevada. I was in critical condition. Nicole, ten years old then, now says, "I really thought this was my final goodbye to you, Mom. I didn't see how you could ever live through this."

I quickly arrived at Washoe Medical Center by helicopter and was admitted as a Trauma Blue[2] patient. Dr. Steven Kennedy[3] headed the emergency room work to assess and help stabilize me. Some X-rays were taken, and a chest tube was inserted. After these procedures, I was immediately taken to the operating room because of the severity of my injuries and bleeding.

I was indeed a fortunate woman because a skilled neurosurgeon, Dr. Jay Morgan[4], happened to be on call that Sunday afternoon. He did over three hours of detailed surgery to carefully remove my epidural hematomas (blood clots pressing on the brain), to decompress and repair some of my skull fractures, and to close my open head wounds with sutures and staples. As part of this complex surgery, Dr. Morgan made craniotomies (holes in both sides of the skull to allow for needed repairs), and he inserted titanium plates, rivets, screws, and then Hemovacs (head tubes for draining). His excellent neurosurgery helped to control the bleeding and swelling that otherwise would have damaged my brain. I later learned that I was fortunate, also, to have an open (bleeding externally) rather than closed head injury. With this type of severe trauma, the bleeding served as a pressure relief valve for my brain during the time between my fall and the neurosurgery.

I had a right hemopneumothorax, a lung collapsed from the pressure of blood and air in my chest cavity. This was not initially seen by X-ray, but Dr. Kennedy wisely had inserted a chest tube in the emergency room, between my right ribs, for drainage and healing. With the force of the fall and multiple broken bones, I had crushed my third and seventh cranial (head) nerves on the right side, so my right eye was completely closed and very swollen. Fortunately, my optic (eye) nerves were intact. I was given two pints of blood, IV fluids, antibiotics, eye ointments, morphine, etc.

I also had ten X-rays and nine CT scans plus an ultrasound from that Sunday through the next seven days. This radiology initially showed 32 fractures in my head and two in my cervical spine at C-6-7 (neck), but they were on the transverse portion, which meant that my spinal cord was OK. As the week progressed I had more detailed CT scans of my head, brain, face, eyes, neck, and abdomen. The CT scans of my head showed cracks that ran into cracks with so many fractures that the radiologist quit naming them specifically and instead wrote: *Multiple, extended, and comminuted skull fractures that also extend to her eye orbits including the sphenoid* (a butterfly shaped bony structure around the base of eyes that also houses the pituitary gland behind the eyes). In other words, my head was cracked, kind of like Humpty Dumpty.

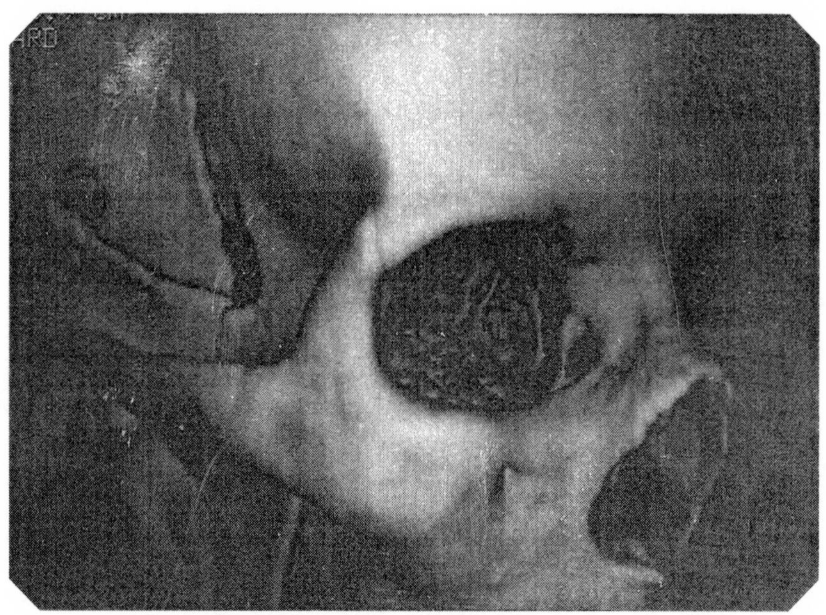

CT Image of my head taken 6 days after accident.

But could the doctors, with all their medical personnel, really put me back together again?

Monday, Carole: swollen face, hands, arms. Bloody turban, right eye swollen shut. Cervical collar. Tubes taped in mouth, drains from every orifice and then some. People about – who? Can't recall. Inside there is a smart, funny, strong, graceful, slender, sparkling beautiful woman. …

Carole is agitated. Reaching to claw out her tubes. Restrain her, talk gently: "Relax Carole, lie down please." She does. The left eye opens and may or may not recognize us. "Are you in pain? Squeeze my hand for yes." Squeeze. Press the button for morphine. Carole drifts away. …

Early Tuesday morning, Carole is conscious, sporadically, but can't yet talk – she's heavily sedated and has a mouth full of tubes. CAT scans are good, and she's making great progress physically. She's responsive to requests – can lift fingers and wiggle toes when asked to do so. Also, there is no sign of paralysis – in fact she's quite active, trying to sit up and rip the tubes out of her mouth, presumably so she can talk at us. We're hoping the respirator might come out later today. The respirator can come out as soon as she breathes reliably in her sleep, which she's not doing yet. I think she recognized me early this morning. …

The pain must be terrible. The invasive tubes, the restraints. I'd be scared to death.

(From my friend Craig's journal, written in Reno, one and two days after my accident.)

2

TRAUMA CARE, ACUTE CARE

◇◇◇◇◇

This has been the hardest chapter for me to write. In fact, I initially skipped it entirely. As I read my book-in-progress to friends and colleagues, we all realized that omitting these 10 days left a confusing hole in my story. Confusion is a normal and disturbing aspect of trauma. What I am sharing here has come from medical records, written records that loved ones kept, and multiple stories shared with me since my accident.

Fears and questions after my accident included:

"What happened?"

"How did it happen?"

"Could it have been prevented?"

"Am I getting all the help I need?"

"How are my family, friends, and clients doing?"

"Will I recover? Will I be OK?"

"Will my loved ones be OK?"

"How will we survive financially as well as physically and emotionally?"

"Will I ever live fully again?"

But these questions were put on hold by morphine, a strong opiate that was given to me by IV (through my veins). I know from a C-section in 1990 that I hate morphine: it makes my brain fuzzy and does not fully cut the pain for me. I have learned since my big ski accident that morphine is the usual drug of choice for severe head injuries because it gives the brain a chance to rest and heal. I was strongly drugged initially in Reno, and I have no memory of my time at Washoe Medical Center. Morphine, head injury, and major trauma can all wipe out memory; I had triple jeopardy.

I was at Washoe Medical Center for 10 days. While in Trauma ICU the first week: my critical condition was stabilized, I had neurosurgery (head/brain) along with a chest tube placement, and I rested and slept. I was never in a coma, though some staff charted that I was, probably because I was very zonked out by heavy drugs and much sleeping. Initially I was intubated and on a respirator, so I was not able to speak. However, from the beginning of my stay at Washoe Medical, I could respond to questions by squeezing with my fingers.

The following descriptions were written in my hospital chart:

Monday April 17, 2000: *the day after her 'skier versus tree' crash and neurosurgery, patient is still feisty and able to communicate nonverbally with the nurse, when not totally sedated by morphine.*

April 17-19: *wrists restrained most of the time, because patient tried to tear the tubes out when awake.* I imagine all the hospital machinery must have felt disturbingly confining to me in my confused state, and in retrospect I realize that my fight for life response was stuck "On" and continued so for several months.

Tuesday April 18: *stood up with assistance, put socks on, and was continuing to respond nonverbally to questions.*

Wednesday April 19: *patient unplugged from the respirator and five tubes removed: endotracheal* (mouth toward lungs for oxygen), *NG* (mouth toward stomach for food), *one of two IVs, and two head drains. Patient could not talk at first because the endotracheal tube made her throat sore, but within hours she began speaking, calling some people by name, and she was happy to be able to eat chocolate again. Patient wanted and tried to get up and walk as soon as possible.*

Thursday April 20: *patient went outside in a wheelchair.*

Friday April 21: *patient had an ophthalmology consultation for her right orbital* (eye bone) *fracture and edema* (swelling). … *No longer on morphine, taking Percocet* (a strong narcotic given by mouth), *one to two pills every three hours as needed for pain.* I know that Percocet does cut the pain for me, and it was probably a tremendous relief finally to feel less pain in my head and body.

Later that day: *patient was able to walk and dialogue with others. The rehab doctors suggested it would be helpful if patient visualized her favorite activities, and by evening she was talking and joking.* How right they were.

CT scans then revealed that I had a left temporal lobe contusion (bruise on the left side of my brain) that did not show up at first because of swelling. In retrospect, this must have been from a coup-contrecoup injury: I hit the tree with the right side of my head, and that slammed the left side of my brain against my skull bones. The swelling and bruising in my brain caused a temporary hemiparesis (nerve/muscular weakening) on the right side of my body that was worse in my right arm than in my right leg, plus some language/cognitive issues. But I was not paralyzed.

Craig described my doctor in his journal: *Morgan, the tall, islander neurosurgeon, quiet, thoughtful, observant, listening and watching for subtle behavioral symptoms.*

Dr. Morgan[1], who actually saw my brain during his neurosurgery, was the only doctor during my post-accident medical process who believed that I could have a full recovery. He saw and charted that the dura (outer lining of my brain) was intact. His surgery had relieved the pressure of blood between my dura and scalp that otherwise would have damaged my brain.

On April 22, 2000, Dr. Morgan wrote the following in my ICU discharge summary: *I think the prognosis is excellent. She probably will take three to six months to get back to her former activity and work as a psychologist.*

I read his note a year later as I went through my medical

records. Piecing together what happened during and after my accident, through records and conversations, was helpful to me in my emotional healing process, as it has been for many other trauma survivors.

On that day, six days after my ski accident, I was no longer in critical condition. I was moved out of the trauma ICU and transferred to a medical-surgical floor of the hospital for acute medical treatment. By then my head attire had changed: *scalp dressing gone; patient wearing a stocking cap to protect head sutures*, and it was reported in my chart: *patient loves foot rubs*. I continued with physical therapy (PT) while in the acute medical unit in Reno, had a rehabilitation medicine consultation, and was prepared by the hospital personnel for transfer to a hospital for inpatient brain injury rehabilitation closer to home.

Unfortunately, at the time of my accident I was a single parent and experiencing painful relational disappointments. I had no primary person, such as a spouse, parent, or adult child, available to deal consistently with the situations created by my accident: my medical problems; my own clients and private practice; financial expenses, losses, and pressures; and most importantly, Nicole's care and wellbeing. I also needed love and support after such a trauma. Fortunately, I rested in a net of close connections and loving support, noted by staff in both Reno and Bay Area hospital records after my accident. It was as if I were flying and missed the trapeze. As I fell, I got in a messy tangle, but the connection of loved ones plus good health habits all my adult life gave me a strong enough safety net. I later heard from loved ones how scary and overwhelming it was to see me in such a condition, and I have heard from their stories about how people shared the tasks of helping both Nicole and me, as well as supporting one another.

In Reno, three close friends and one of my brothers arrived within the first day; another brother arrived before the next weekend. My friend Margaret[2], who was On Call for me to cover my private practice during my planned for vacation to Paris, came right away. Friends Jerry and Craig also came to support and help me. Craig, a friend I met heli-skiing in Canada in 1987, broadened information sharing and support for me through email and the Internet. Craig also held my hand, rubbed my back and feet, provided his loving, gentle, encouraging presence that I needed, felt, and appreciated. Jerry and Craig took turns being at my side all the time during that first week of my post-accident hospital stay. Jerry began organizing logistics of who would help with which areas of my life.

My brother Jim[3] arrived within a day, to help oversee my medical care, and my brother Dave[4] arrived on Friday; both brought me in-person family love and support. Jim, a fireman, EMT-I, and psychotherapist, was assigned by Jerry to notify our large extended family about my accident.

After years of working for a Texas fire department, Jim later described his experience of me in Reno: "I have seen multiple head injuries in my work: falls, motorcycle and other accidents. I wanted to be optimistic and was praying. I didn't expect you to be yourself, even if you survived. Knowing you probably would not survive, given the accident you had, I flew immediately to Reno to see you. I saw a level of injury to your head that I had never seen anyone survive. By five days after I got there, you woke up and were surprisingly alert and able to talk appropriately. You recognized me, found words, called me by name, thanked me for coming to help, and told me that your head hurt. You did not have the level of brain dysfunction that is often present with less traumatic injury. Only then did I believe that I was not losing my sister."

Family and friends wrote, visited, and called me, reaching out with love and support. Many people were praying for me. I later heard of shamanic rituals that were sent my way shortly after I crashed into that tree, with a focus on saving my life. Other friends were meditating and visualizing full healing for me. I was sent emotional and spiritual help from many directions.

By report, I had lucid conversations with friends—by phone and in person in Reno—after I was extubated (breathing tube removed). I asked about specific events that I remembered were occurring in friends' lives. I called people by name. I was vocal with anger and upset about some relationship pains. Again, I have no memory of any of these conversations and was surprised to hear about them in such detail later.

For instance, shortly after I was extubated, a ski friend came to see me for his first hospital visit. Upon seeing him, my first post-accident words were a casual, "Hi, Tim."

My friend Susan has told me that when we first spoke by phone, I asked, "When do you leave on your vacation? I hope you have a great time." I had remembered that she was going on a cruise with part of her extended family. My brain was working just fine in some ways.

Sadly, Nicole's father had not been a part of her life for a while, which made the thought of losing her mother even more terrifying. She was very worried about where she would land after my fall in that fateful ski race.

Meanwhile, as I later found out, Nicole spent her spring break in Carson City, Nevada, making daily trips to visit me at the hospital in Reno, instead of her expected vacation in Paris. Until she had to return to school, Nicole stayed with the family of Donna, my close ski friend. Nicole also got help, support, and transportation from other ski team friends, who lived in Carson City/Minden or part time in the nearby Sierra Nevada Mountains. This wider net was good for Nicole, because people close to a traumatized person are often in such shock themselves that they forget to tune into the needs of children.

Nicole was in a state of psychological trauma. At first she thought I was dying. I was her main safety net, and now my own safety and life were unclear to her. Nicole later told me that she worried about whether I would ever be able to take care of her again, and if not, who would.

I tried to express love to Nicole with my eyes and arms while intubated and, as soon as I could talk, verbally. She was naturally frightened by the intense hospital environment and by my appearance.

Emotionally, my accident was more traumatic for Nicole than it was for me. I was 48 and engaged in recovery, whereas Nicole was only 10 and felt profoundly helpless as a result of my accident. It can be harder for a loved one to observe trauma than for the injured one to endure it. This is particularly true for children because they are dependent and they do not yet have a solid sense of who they are.

Sadly, children are often kept aside when a parent is ill, injured, dying, or dead. And that is a crucial time when children need more patient listening, help, and love than ever. Yet often they are related to as if a nuisance. I have heard many such stories over the years in my work as a psychologist. The long term impact of this can feel truly devastating and then complicate development of a sense of self that is both independent and connected to others.

I have heard that many of our loved ones did their best to reach out to Nicole by listening, providing positive distractions, attending to her basic needs, and expressing concern and care. Yet Nicole later said, "Mom, I felt totally alone. I did *not* get the help I needed."

Nicole was actually afraid of being orphaned by the turn of events in our Orphaned Female Family Team relay ski race. In a moment, she went from her thrill of speed and her part of a race well done to the trauma of potentially losing her mother. It has taken years for Nicole and me to work through her trauma as fully as possible (more about that in Chapter 17).

I learned that at the end of her spring vacation, on Sunday April 23, 2000, one week after my accident, Nicole was driven back to

Berkeley by our friend Jerry, who also lives there. In Berkeley, Nicole stayed with close women friends, Marilee[5] and Lois and their families, while she returned to 4th Grade at Berkeley Arts Magnet School. I was to be transferred to a Bay Area hospital for inpatient rehabilitation within a few days.

Meanwhile in Reno, my family and friends all had to leave around the time Nicole did. On April 23 it was charted in my hospital record that I had *some mental confusion related to low blood sodium* and that *this cleared up quickly with an IV correction.*

By report, I was *most irrational on Monday April 24.* It was presumed that I had *too many visitors on Saturday and Sunday,* so visitation numbers were kept more restricted for me until my final discharge from rehab on May 12. In retrospect, I believe it is just as likely that I felt terrified, sad, and lonely because my daughter, brothers, and close friends had suddenly all left; I no longer had a stream of loved ones by my side.

Fortunately, my ski and mountain friends from the Tahoe/Carson City area continued to visit every day while I was still in Reno. I spoke with Nicole daily by phone after her return to Berkeley. And I was very excited about returning to the Bay Area myself. In fact, while in Reno, I chose the Bay Area hospital for inpatient rehabilitation over other options because I wanted to be near Berkeley, our home. There I had Nicole, friends, my regular healthcare providers, and my full life, including my practice as a psychologist.

Hooray, I'm going home! Well, at least to the Bay Area, and I hope to be home really soon.

Oh God, "I feel so broke up, I wanna go home." …

(My lament—"Sloop John B" lyrics, 1966, The Beach Boys—emerged from the recesses of my brain as I endured the flight and ambulance rides back to Northern California.)

Into Rehab

Even though friends later told me about conversations we had while I was in the Reno hospital, my first sustained and clear memory after my accident was of my transfer on the medical airplane between Reno, Nevada, and the Bay Area in California, April 26, 2000.

I remember looking around and seeing all the medical equipment in the plane, being a bit confused as I asked, "Where are we going?"

I smiled at the flight medic's reply, "You're going to a Bay Area hospital for inpatient rehabilitation, back to Northern California." Nicole was already in school after spring break, and I missed her. What a relief to be moving toward home. I felt happy.

So, in the ten days after my big ski accident, I was taken first to the clinic at the ski resort, then to the hospital where I was received from helicopter Flight for Life into the ER, to surgery, to a Trauma ICU for a week, and then to a normal acute medical unit. I was ready for an inpatient brain rehabilitation program. I was transferred by ambulance to the airport in Reno, medical air taxi from Reno to the Bay Area, then by ambulance to the hospital for inpatient rehabilitation. I was no longer in critical condition, but my body was too fragile to tolerate a four-hour ambulance ride.

The Bay Area hospital for inpatient brain rehabilitation had private hospital rooms, a large room for meals and mingling of patients, plus private conference and meeting rooms. There was a multidisciplinary staff for post-acute assessment and rehabilitation, including physicians and nurses with specialty training in rehabilitation medicine, neuropsychologists, physical therapists, occupational therapists, speech therapists, recreational and respiratory therapists, registered dieticians, and social workers. There was a structured, coordinated rehab program, theoretically designed to improve a patient's ability to perform daily living tasks.

My experience at this hospital for rehabilitation was nothing like my sense of what I needed and hoped to receive. Throughout my stay, no staff person asked me about my needs or wishes, though some nurses listened well and helped me in gentle, kind, tuned in ways. The rehab staff decided what my individual goals should be.

As a nurse who worked at several Bay Area hospitals in the 1970s and 80s, I can say this hospital used to be excellent, with a primary focus on patient treatment and care. However, many once excellent hospitals are struggling to survive upheaval in the American medical system. So I can now see that my challenges with the Bay Area hospital for inpatient rehabilitation were partially caused by the broader problem of healthcare delivery and costs in our country.

But there was also a conflict between my needs and how the rehab team saw me. I learned from my experience that rehab teams often see patients according to how they expect brain-injured patients to recover. I experienced what Harvard-trained brain scientist Jill Bolte Taylor later wrote after her own brain trauma: "I wanted my doctors to focus on how my brain was working rather than on whether it worked according to their criteria or timetable."[1]

I was surprised to read recently in my Reno hospital record (charted April 25, 2000, the day before my transport to the Bay Area) that a rehab prep caseworker told my family and charted:

Carole might need to be in a group living situation, perhaps in a hospital, for up to a year. Dr. Morgan[2] *meant that she would be out of work for at least six months. Make plans for the care of Nicole, because Carole might never again be able to work as a psychologist.* Interesting that the rehab caseworker reframed and changed what the neurosurgeon wrote and said to my family and close friends.

I am thankful that this poor prognosis was never told to me in Reno. It perhaps influenced the formation of the staff's view of me at the Bay Area hospital for inpatient rehabilitation—very different from what my Reno neurosurgeon wrote and said. In fact, I now wonder if the Bay Area rehab team even read my neurosurgeon's reports, assessments, and suggestions, because close friends had to remind the Bay Area rehab staff to follow-up on specific concerns seen by my neurosurgeon, including my right eye.

Regardless of the cause, I longed for the rehab staff to be interested in and to ask me about my needs and wishes, even when they thought that I could not think clearly. We all need listening and patience, especially when we are patients. I have learned over the 41 years since I became a registered nurse and the 32 years since I became a licensed psychologist that we each are unique in our capacities, strengths, vulnerabilities, difficulties, and healing needs and process. It is amazing what people can and will articulate when asked and heard.

(The confusing letter below, quoted as written, was given to me five days after my arrival, while I was still taking narcotics, based on testing done while I was on narcotics. Written by the neuropsychologist assigned to me in the Bay Area hospital for inpatient rehabilitation, my name was spelled incorrectly.)

Dear Carol,

Since your arrival ..., I have had the opportunity to learn about your exceptional skills as a clinician and athlete. I have learned about your empathy, sensitivity and devotion to helping others. Here on the rehabilitation unit, we are devoted to helping you to work towards regaining your skills. Due to difficulty with your memory, I am writing the following to help you to understand and recall the current details of your medical status.

... (description of accident and Reno medical help, transfer to Bay Area) ...

The brain injury team has evaluated you and the results of the initial assessment follow.

Physically, you are able to move all your limbs with some decreased strength in both arms. You have frequent and persistent headaches, lower back and posterior pain. You often feel dizzy when sitting up after being prone for a while. Your right eyelid will not open voluntarily due to the 3rd nerve injury.

The largest impact of your brain injury is on your cognitive and memory skills. You currently show a pattern of cognitive difficulties that is very typical for individuals who have suffered injuries to the frontal and temporal lobes. You currently are having difficulty with expressive language, verbal memory and verbal reasoning. Your complex attention skills and cognitive processing speed are diminished.

The most significant problem at present is that you appear unaware of these cognitive problems and the functional impact of the cognitive deficits from your brain injury. You are unable to notice the errors you make and thus cannot correct them. As is common with frontal lobe injuries, you at times show a disconnection between your thinking in the current moment and your actions at a later time. Thus you can state a reasonable course of action, but you may not execute the action later.

The brain injury team has set the following goals for you:

1) *To improve your deficit awareness ...*
2) *To address issues of safety, we will work with you to have you achieve the ability to get up and ambulate safely with in (sic) your room.*
3) *To address your difficulty with communication ...*
4) *To address your memory difficulties, we will work with you to learn and to be able to express the nature and functional impact of the cognitive deficits due to your head injury.*

... Once I have reviewed this information with you, I will leave this letter with you to help you to review these facts about your case.

(signed with phone number of neuropsychologist)

4

Out of the Cage: Overcoming Problems in the Rehab Unit

In the rehab unit, I first experienced the impact of what I call the "brain injury grid."[1] I now understand that I was seen in a formulaic way for patients with my sort of head injury: brain injured and presumably incapable of wise, independent thinking; in denial about my injury; and disinhibited, i.e. unable to talk and behave in socially acceptable, emotionally restrained ways. It was assumed that my independent life would cease, because I was deemed no longer capable of complex problem solving. Hence, I would probably no longer function as a psychologist nor be able to run my own household. Doctors at the rehab unit called in my family, friends, and colleagues, with a focus on my limitations and how to "manage Carole," the feisty brain-injured geek, the former athlete who could no longer be trusted to be physically safe with her own body. It was all about controlling me from the outside, for my safety and the safety of others.

Though I was struggling to integrate and accept my traumatized condition, I wanted to have as much independence *and* help as possible. Within six days of admittance to the hospital for inpatient rehabilitation, I understood and began remembering that I was still in an acute post-injured state. Not hard to see, given

I had a shaved and dented head with hardened dark dried blood around metal staples, fresh scars from a long laceration down the right side of my face, and two black eyes, one of them swollen and completely closed. Not hard to feel, given the severe aches and pains in my body.

I wanted to be treated with respect, and I wanted to heal. Fortunately, some family and friends helped soften the rough edges of my inpatient rehab experience.

As a nurse and a psychologist, I understand how hospitals work, I understand good treatment of patients, and I understand the emotional sequelae after trauma. Also, I had studied neuropsychology for three years during my PhD training. This all helped me navigate the brain injury grid rehab experience. I share it now to help others who might be in a similar situation. How I was being treated in the rehab unit caused me to rage behind closed doors about the medical establishment and healthcare system; it fueled my desire to write this book.

To begin with, when I was admitted to my inpatient rehab room, I was put in a Vail bed, the hospital equivalent of a zoo cage. This type of bed is totally enclosed. Designed to keep a patient in, it is often used for patients who cannot be trusted to be cooperative. Waking up to this confinement of bars felt claustrophobic and unsettling. It also felt unnecessary, confusing, and frightening when I emerged from sleep after having been admitted to the rehab unit and drugged with narcotics. I hated it, and I protested, "Why are you locking me in like this?"

I was told, "This is necessary because you got out of bed unaccompanied in Reno and fell. You are at risk of injuring yourself further."

"Oh," I replied, as I understood why I was put in the cage. But I believed it was no longer necessary. I spoke up, "I promise that I will call for help if you put me in a normal bed."

The staff did not agree, "We can't do that. You might forget to call, and we are concerned about your safety."

So I bargained: "How about if we try the following: I use my call button, and you respond quickly when I need to go to the bathroom? If I do this well for a full day, then put me in a regular hospital bed with side rails up. If I continue to call each time I need to get up for another day, allow the side rails to be put down when I am awake, and I promise to still call for assistance. If I fail at any of these goals, keep me in the Vail bed."

"We can give this a try," the staff reluctantly agreed, probably certain that I would be unable to remember this plan and keep my agreement.

I succeeded. I felt relieved and happy to get out of the cage.

Another big problem was the food. Food actually provides the building blocks of our cells, our bodies. I eat very healthy food normally, and the hospital food was disgusting to me. I wondered to myself, *How can people heal on such food*? This is often a problem with institutional food.

I craved salads, fresh fruit, non-greasy lightly cooked fish. Fortunately, my daughter, aided by our friends, blessed me with delicious salads and fresh fruits, plus sushi, chocolate, and many goodies brought straight from farmers' markets and fresh produce grocery stores.

My next big problem was extreme aching in my body, including a very sore butt from lying in bed so much. My normally active body was flipping out from this sedentary hospital lifestyle on top of a nasty sports injury and surgery.

Years ago, I had imagined that one day if I got rich, I would love to have a weekly massage. A few years before my big ski accident, I read an article in the *American Psychologist* (Journal of the American Psychological Association) that reviewed studies on the therapeutic benefits of massage.[2] Massage therapy was shown to provide physical and emotional benefits for many conditions. That made it easier to justify this treat: for my health rather than just for pleasure, I could afford a weekly therapeutic massage.

My friend Joan Provencher[3] had been providing me with regular professional massages for a fee for several years. When Joan arrived at the rehab unit, she was told, "You can *not* bring a massage table to Carole's room because you do *not* have hospital privileges," though Joan was planning to give me a free gift of massage while I was in the hospital.

Give me a break, I thought. *How can people heal without touch, without physically as well as nutritionally supporting their bodies?*

I said, "I could sign a waiver. I'm in a private room."

"No, it's against hospital policy."

After Joan returned her portable massage table to her truck, we figured out how to deal with this hospital rule: Joan came to the inpatient rehab unit daily and massaged me as I lay on my side and back, in my hospital bed. Then later after hospital discharge, she massaged me on her portable massage table at my home, gradually less frequently, until I was able to resume our regular weekly appointments in Joan's massage studio.

I was now receiving complementary physical and emotional help. Daily massage helped my aching body. Good food did more than just taste yummy; it helped my body recover and feel strengthened from the inside. Visits and calls from friends and family helped me stay connected with my net of relationships. Friends also helped me laugh, which felt good and offered positive perspective. With my own fighting spirit, I had negotiated my way out of the bed cage, moved and walked more, and I strengthened physically as I did so. As psychologist and philosopher Paul Watzlawick titled his book: *The Situation Is Hopeless, But Not Serious.*[4] I continued to work with positive visualizations, as suggested by the rehab doctors in Reno. Also, I was being prayed for and I prayed.

As I now reflect on my hospital for inpatient rehabilitation experience, I can see from notes in my hospital chart that I was indeed fighting to be seen for my full, prior self, plus striving to prepare for return to work and my former life. From the vantage point of somatic therapy, my fight or flight response to a severely traumatic accident was clearly stuck in the On position at the rehab unit. I now understand that I was indeed a handful and am grateful that my self-preservation instinct helped me navigate these disconcerting experiences. I developed this understanding years later, after I studied somatic therapy. It would have been wonderful if the rehab staff had understood—and helped me to understand—that my behavior was related at least in part to my injured instinctive fight for life and not only a symptom of my brain injury.

I am disturbed that you had the experience you did while being a patient in a brain injury rehab unit. Any good neuropsychologist is trained also as a good clinician. It is ridiculous to do testing on a patient taking opiates. Brain functioning in the immediate aftermath of a head injury is altered and often changes, so this is a poor time to make predictions of future functioning. It is necessary to talk to patients with compassion and encouragement, as any good clinician would. Unconscionable.

(As explained to me several months after my inpatient discharge, by friend and colleague Brenda Townes, PhD, neuropsychologist, Professor Emeritus, Department of Psychiatry and Behavioral Sciences, University of Washington School of Medicine.[1])

5

Oh, My Head ...

Then there was the problem of my brain injury, including struggles with short-term memory. The neuropsychologist assigned to me was the closest peer on the rehab unit to me as a psychologist. He presumably did objective measures, yet he most misjudged me. When I was first given intelligence and neuropsych tests at the Bay Area hospital for inpatient rehabilitation shortly after my arrival from Reno, while still on opiates, I raged internally and thought: *Give me a break.* Yet I tried to do my best and to be cooperative, even when I wanted to sleep and felt like refusing to cooperate.

Apparently I succeeded, given the hospital charting. For instance, the day after my admission, the neuropsychologist wrote after testing me: *She shows ability to respond politely and makes good effort on tests administered.*

I was tested to assess the extent of the impact of my head injury on my brain functioning. Not right, not a fair assessment, given the timing. Even now as I read the "Progress Record" entries made by this neuropsychologist from my admission to discharge in this hospital for inpatient rehabilitation, it makes my blood boil. It is clear that the staff's impressions of me—based on both my memory of what was said to me as well as their charting about me—were dictated by the neuropsychologist's view, until some of the staff got to know me individually.

It is also clear, from reading my hospital chart, that the neuropsychologist was seeking corroboration of a formulated view of me from my friends and colleagues. A few close friends and colleagues later explained to me that they felt intimidated and overwhelmed. Here are some examples:

"I'm so sorry. The neuropsychologist spoke with such authority that I figured he must be correct. I just wanted to be helpful. And I was very worried about you."

"I felt overwhelmed when I first saw you. I wanted my beloved friend Carole back, and I was afraid you might never be you again."

"When I told the neuropsychologist that you were doing well, remembering and thinking better and better, my words fell on deaf ears. It seemed like the neuropsychologist's main goals were to be right and to rein you in, that your natural feistiness was seen as a danger, for others as well as yourself. You've been a feisty one as long as I've known you."

Early in my stay at the rehab center, I kept hoping that my situation was a nightmare: that I would wake up and find my life as usual. We psychologists call this denial. It is one of the ways the body-mind often tries to cope emotionally with trauma.

One afternoon, five days after my arrival in the Bay Area hospital for inpatient rehabilitation (fifteen days after my accident), my friend Margaret[2] was visiting me again, providing love and emotional support. When asked, Margaret, crying, told me the accident story yet again, adding: "In the Reno hospital, you were covered in white bandages, literally wrapped from head to toe. You also had multiple tubes coming out of your body. Lying in bed, in white sheets. Looking pretty lifeless. Then, it was as if you were Lazarus, arose from the dead, walked, and then talked again."

Her tears and this powerful image made quite an impression on me. Because of these strong associated emotions, this story now stayed in my memory. Emotions and images do enhance memory capacity.

I decided to investigate my memory problem. The next time a nurse brought pills to me when I was awake, I asked, "What is this?"

"A little something to help you with your pain."

Knowing that narcotics dull memory, I asked, "What is it specifically? A narcotic?"

"Well, yes. It's Vicodin."

I then asked, "Is this a p.r.n. order?"

"Yes, it is."

P.r.n. is the Latin abbreviation for *pro re nata*, meaning as circumstances may require. This is sometimes used in prescription writing, and it means as needed/requested by a patient, up to a maximal amount and frequency for safety.

I then challenged her with, "I did not ask for it, did I?"

She replied, "You need it. You will have intolerable pain if you do not take it. We are trying to help you.

"I would rather have pain and a brain, my brain functioning back, than no pain and no brain. I refuse this medicine, and please put in my chart that I will no longer take narcotics."

I was grateful that I am a nurse myself and know how the medication systems in hospitals work. I am also an addictions expert who understands the impact of narcotics on brain functioning.

My refusal of narcotics had a huge and multifaceted fallout, tough but ultimately good. My head pain was indeed horrific; it felt as if my brain would literally explode. But, having grown up with three brothers, I am tough and decided to endure this. And thankfully my rehab doctor had prescribed a non-narcotic medicine that was begun the day before Margaret's emotional visit: Neurontin, which is an anticonvulsant and analgesic (pain reliever).

Soon after my refusal of narcotics, a relatively mild prescription medicine to relieve tension and vascular headaches, Midrin, was prescribed p.r.n. I took Midrin in place of Vicodin as needed. The combination of Neurontin and Midrin took the worst edge off my severe head pain. I did not take Vicodin again until a year later when I needed it in the acute phase after an eye surgery that was related to this accident.

As I contemplated my pain experience while writing this chapter, I realized in retrospect that I must have been going through some sort of withdrawal syndrome, because the worst of the acute brain splitting pain subsided within a few days as my body and brain adapted to having no narcotics. After recalling this experience, I was amazed to find the amount of Vicodin I was given in my hospital chart: up to two pills five times a day at the rehab center, probably in response to being asked to rate my pain level and in response to my groans of pain. I remember that the pain was worse when I was confined to bed than when I was up and mobile. I never directly asked for Vicodin. The Midrin was given either two or three times a day, as I asked for it. The Neurontin, prescribed twice a day and at bedtime, was not a p.r.n. medicine. This abrupt change in medicines confirms that I must have gone through withdrawal when I stopped taking narcotics cold turkey after frequent doses for sixteen days, begun in ICU and continued until I refused narcotics after my emotional talk with Margaret.

I was also stunned to see in my hospital chart that there was nothing written about my refusal of narcotics. In addition, there was no record of the positive and negative correlates of this notable change in medications and pain management. Improvements were noted by the nurses, starting the day after I stopped opiates, with no apparent awareness of this correlation—until each time I spoke up about it—and never charted as correlated.

From my training as a nurse and my work as a clinical psychologist, I know how important it is to chart: 1) any addition or deletion of narcotics or other mind-altering drugs taken by a patient, 2) the reason for and impact of the change, and 3) to note sensation, pain, behavioral, mental, and emotional changes that appear to be correlated in time with the medication change. All of these observations and communications can greatly improve patient understanding and care.

Mind-altering drugs can help with pain and healing, when given at the right dose and time. For instance, Percocet really helped me in Reno, when I got off the Morphine. But mind-altering drugs can slow healing and recovery when given too much or for too long. When masking pain becomes a primary goal, there is a cost in capacity to function and internal sense of wellbeing. There are many alternatives to narcotics including: relaxation techniques, imagery work, hypnosis and self-hypnosis, working with thought processes, cognitive behavioral therapy, biofeedback, neurostimulation therapy, Somatic Experiencing®, somatic therapy, body psychotherapies, and body therapies.[3]

My brain felt as if I were living in a dense fog before I stopped the narcotics. I especially wondered if I was really a goner and done for mentally after my emotional conversation with Margaret. I finally remembered this conversation after Margaret's many previous attempts to let me know what had happened to me—because of her vivid imagery of how I had looked in Reno and because she was crying, which upset me. I viewed my stopping the narcotics as a kind of experiment—to see if my memory and other problems were exacerbated by narcotics or if this was all a result of my head injury. I intuited that the meds were clouding my mind. Narcotics do that, and it made sense to me that this would occur even more so after a severe head injury. But I cannot help wondering what would have happened to me if I had given in to the view of me that was held by the rehab staff, if I had lacked the training and experience to challenge their perceptions and to change the course of my treatment and healing. A knowledgeable health advocate could be another solution for this kind of healthcare conundrum.

Wednesday night, May 3

Rejoice! Carole has been told that she'll be discharged from the hospital on May 16. This is great news, and she's very excited about getting back home and seeing friends again.

The cervical collar came off today, and was replaced with a soft foam collar to help stabilize the neck. It's much more comfortable!

Carole is fully conscious and quite lucid. … We talked a lot about the future.

Onward!

Craig (from his journal)

Nurse Flowsheet

May 1, 2000: Able to do Hygiene care with set up assistance only.

May 3, 2000: Cleared for Independent transfers/ambulation in room - doing well. Safety awareness improved. Increased awareness of deficits. Emotional reassurance given. Patient involved in decision making. Expressed concerns and fears about daughter's care.

May 4, 2000: Able to attend to tasks at hand…. Improving ability to deal with more complex issues – planned home care of daughter.

Neuropsychology Progress Record

May 3, 2000: Patient alert, able to accurately report change from hard to soft collar and that MRI showed no structural problems in lower back. She recalled OT activity for organizing cooking activity. She indicated she had little interest in cooking even though she says she is an excellent cook. Her main focus is return to work … (neuropsychologist then listed all of his concerns about that).

May 4, 2000: Reviewed patient's cognitive changes in attention, language, memory and most significantly lack of awareness of deficits and ability to think about her status in the abstract.

May 8, 2000: … Her daily recall is much improved. She reports visits on Saturday. … Patient better at staying on task in discussion today. Emotional expression better controlled as well.

6

Post-Narcotic Rapid Recovery

As I was no longer zoned out on narcotics, my behavior in the rehab unit started changing rapidly, to the dismay of some of the staff. This made me a challenging, difficult patient in their eyes. My changes were somewhat noted in my hospital chart and not connected to the medication change.

I stopped taking Vicodin the morning of May 2, 2000, and my hospital records documented the following:

May 3: *able to ambulate independently in room* (written by nurses); *slightly increased memory* (written by neuropsychologist);

May 4: *improved attention and focus, ability to deal with more complex issues, improving memory/learning* (written by nurses); this same day the neuropsychologist gathered what information he could from outside parties to corroborate his view of my lack of awareness, safety, and insight due to my brain injured status—I know this because it was well-documented in my chart. I do not recall ever giving the neuropsychologist permission to do this, and there was no signed document of permission in my hospital chart.

The neuropsychologist's failure to understand what was going on in my brain's healing process was disconcerting to me. I was pleased with my rapid recovery, the best possible outcome from my experiment of refusing the mind-altering drugs. My brain was working, but I was still in pain and injured, still needing time to heal.

I was doing my best to escape the brain injury grid. That was difficult because some of the rehab staff (and some of my colleagues and friends) accepted the neuropsychologist's assessment completely. So instead of recognizing my rapid improvements in memory and brain functioning, they kept looking for clues to support a view of the expectable outcome of my injury. What I really needed now was support for the changes I was experiencing, including enduring the head pain from being off narcotics.

It also would have helped to be encouraged about my improving physical capacities. For instance, I became so adept at the physical therapy exercises that my physical therapists did not know what to do with me. One said, "I have nothing more to offer you here. You can do everything well, and I feel helpless to improve your physical status now."

"Don't worry. I would love to go outside for a long walk, to get fresh air and stretch my legs. I miss running."

So I began taking daily 45-minute walks with physical therapists in the residential and business neighborhoods near the Bay Area hospital for inpatient rehabilitation, a little over one week after I arrived. I loved being outside—breathing the fresh air, seeing many brightly colored flowers and green trees. These walks helped me feel alive and connected to the blossoming of springtime, to the world, to Northern California, as well as to my own body and its very gradually returning strength. I also noticed that my strength and balance were definitely not as good as before my accident.

I loved the walking, but I missed running. I began running when I was in middle school, doing track and field, competing in races. In my early 20s, I read Kenneth Cooper's *Aerobics*.[1] Dr. Cooper did the first extensive medical research on the health benefits of aerobic exercise, studying Air Force cadets. Given all the diseases that ran in my extended family, which could be mitigated by regular aerobic exercise (i.e. glaucoma, varicose veins, adult onset diabetes, hypertension, etc.), I decided immediately after reading *Aerobics* that I would continue running, which at that time was considered the simplest way of getting aerobic exercise. I also wanted to stay in shape for the mountain sports I loved, understanding from Dr. Cooper's book that conditioning would be needed to support my body in the process of aging. I have been running four to six days a week since I first read *Aerobics* in 1976. I am certain this is one of the reasons I survived my ski accident: I had ample collateral circulation, good muscular strength, and an attuned sense of my body. All this helped in my fight for life in that tree well. I forever will be grateful to Dr. Cooper for his pioneering research and book. Because I took his research seriously, I am alive and well as a middle-aged woman, despite my bodily traumas.

My memory and capacity to express myself improved rapidly after I was off narcotics, probably also aided by the positive effects of exercising, eating nutritious food, and feeling loved by those closest to me.

I was furious about how I and other rehab patients were being talked to and treated. So I spoke up.

Many of the rehab staff could not believe my change and how quickly my memory improved after stopping the narcotics. Instead of believing what I told them, they assumed that I was making things up, confabulating (what brain injured people do unconsciously to fill in their memory gaps). Because I felt frustrated and angry about not being believed, the staff then considered me disinhibited (socially inappropriate because of my head injury).

I laugh at the irony when I recall how misunderstood I often felt while an inpatient for brain injury rehabilitation. Though I spoke up some of the time, the staff had no idea that I actually chose where, when, how, and with whom I expressed my anger once I was off the narcotics. I never let the depth of my feelings verbally rip in front of or with the rehab staff.

I expressed my frustrations to the staff in a somewhat professional, quite civilized way. Compared to the intensity of my inner feelings, I was subdued when I told them about my concerns, because I wanted to be seen for my current self, and I wanted to get out of the hospital as quickly as possible. It had become clear to me that direct expression of anger by all the brain-injured patients in this rehab unit was seen as disinhibition. I did not believe that label should be applied to me now, once I was off narcotics. I have heard enough stories from friends who visited me in Reno to know that I was indeed disinhibited verbally when I was strongly drugged on narcotics early in my acute hospital recovery process. Opiates, like alcohol and other central nervous system depressants, cause disinhibition, even without a head injury. Witness people who drink alcohol to loosen up socially, for example.

I made certain that I could not be heard when I vented in muted tones behind closed doors. I instinctively felt the need to let my inner agitation out, when I felt enraged about being misunderstood. I appreciated those trusted close friends who listened to my feelings. I still have detailed memories of my anger expression choices during my post-narcotic rapid recovery process. For instance, Craig listened well when we talked on the phone, behind closed doors, so I shared openly with him. Craig's journal entry May 3: "Lovely long talk with Carole. Feeling very close. Proud to be feisty, she fulminates for over an hour, about specific people. She's able to ask pointed questions now and can understand why she's so angry and when she may have been unfair."

As Joan—who climbed mountains in the Himalayas with me and knows me well—said in private, "Carole uses strong words when she's pissed off or really scared. She did this before this accident. She's direct about her anger. This is Carole; it's not brain injury disinhibition. She has specific reasons to be angry. And anyway, it's human to let off steam when angry. We all do it one way or the other."[2]

I was angry: about the pain and losses caused by my accident; about the disruption of my life; and about how I was not being seen for the real me at the rehab center. I was also angry about the decline in the quality of healthcare in our country and its effect on my hospital inpatient rehab experience. I wanted to write this book: to help trauma survivors and all patients to tune into their bodies and ask family and friends as well as true healers for help as needed; and to encourage healthcare providers and other helping professionals to ask, listen to, see, respect, and care about their patients/clients.

Anger can be a good sign in the post-trauma recovery process. As physician Rachel Naomi Remen wrote: "Anger is just a demand for change, a passionate wish for things to be different. It can be a way to reestablish important boundaries and assert personal integrity in the face of a body- and life-altering disease. And, as it was for me, it may be the first expression of the will to live." Remen also wrote, and I agree, that anger is only a problem when it becomes a way of life. It can be a positive response to suffering and "Eventually it may show us the freedom of loving and serving life…."[3]

The neuropsychologist assigned to me in the hospital for inpatient rehabilitation finally charted details about my improved memory and better-controlled expressions of emotions four to five days after my improvements were charted by nurses. However, even after I had stopped opiates and my thinking and memory improvements had been noted, the neuropsychologist came to my room and told me that I could no longer handle complex problem solving (another task of the frontal and prefrontal cortex).

I disagreed, and I spoke up: "Just last night, after 9, my daughter Nicole awakened me by phoning. She was crying, afraid of a relative who was staying at home with her. She experienced this person as angry with her, and scary. Nicole feared she might be slapped after they had an argument, and she was sobbing as she shared her feelings with me.

"Even while I was waking up from a deep sleep, I quickly scanned the options in my brain. I could send a close family friend to our home, to be present for Nicole that night and help her feel protected and safe. When I offered this option, Nicole expressed relief, 'Yes, Mommy. Thank you.'

"After that, I made more phone calls and arranged for Nicole to stay with Lois, our dear friend who was Nicole's preschool teacher and 'second mother,' after school tomorrow and for a couple more nights until my hospital discharge. I also arranged transportation for Nicole between Lois's house on Hopkins Street and Berkeley Arts Magnet where Nicole goes to school. I think this was complex problem solving, especially given Nicole's strong upset emotions and my own exhausted state that was even worse because I was roused from deep sleep."

As I told the neuropsychologist this story, he seemed unimpressed. I imagine he thought I was confabulating, or at least exaggerating the story. I was relieved about my renewed mental capacity to do that complex problem solving. I wanted to be a good and helpful mother for my daughter. I wished for support and encouragement of my success in being able to help her feel safe, not quiet disbelief. *Oh well, he can't really hear and understand me*, I thought, yet did not say.

I was also upset by how brusquely some other patients in the rehab unit were being treated, without kindness or listening attention. For instance, one woman was making requests and obviously agitated about being ignored. I asked her what was wrong, listened, and then spoke on her behalf to the staff. I was told that she had had multiple head injuries from riding bicycles without a helmet, and could never remember what she was told. I said to the staff, "Listening to her concerns with compassion would go a long way, as would empathy for her struggles and experience."

This woman was clearly able to remember something: I listened to her in a caring way, and she continued to seek me out. Soon, patients wanted to sit by me in the dining area, talking about their problems. Some tried to drop by my private hospital room to get a listening ear or help from me. They saw that I was willing to speak up to the staff.

I know from my own feelings plus the experience of relating to other patients on the rehab unit that patients in distress need to be listened to, asked their concerns and aims, treated with kindness and compassion – basic human decency. These things help emotional and physical healing. But I was exhausted from my accident, needing huge amounts of rest and sleep to allow my body to heal. I knew I could not take on the task of being the unit psychotherapist, so I spent more time in my room with the door closed.

I felt relief and gratitude for my post-narcotic rapid recovery. I also longed for my rehab staff to understand that rapid progress after stopping mind-altering drugs can be genuine and not necessarily just confabulation. It would have been wonderful had the staff recognized and then helped me to understand this experience. It was painful to sort it out alone.

I stared into the mirror and saw my image: head shaved with several long fresh scars including one running down the right side of my face, staples holding portions of my scalp together, black bruises under my eyes and elsewhere, my right eye completely closed and swollen. I was still shocked to see myself looking like this. I joked with myself as a means of coping: "Truly the height of loveliness. Or perhaps a punker's dream image?"

At home for the first time in three weeks, I had begged for a pass from the Bay Area hospital for inpatient rehabilitation. The words of the hospital staff were echoing in my head: "You may never practice psychology again (and we think that may destroy your sense of self). You may never ski again. You may never live independently again. You may have to sell your home and live in a facility for brain injured people." Being home, I could see that my house and plants were a bit neglected. I had indeed been gone as long as the calendar indicated, which I did not want to believe. Being home made it all the more undeniable.

I looked out my front picture window, blessed by the beautiful view of San Francisco and the Golden Gate Bridge. It was a sunny, clear day.

I looked again into the mirror. Here I clearly saw the results of what I had been through. As I looked at my bruised reflected image, I said out loud to myself, "This is not my life."

I again scanned my home, the resplendent view of the San Francisco Bay, the memories of all I love and cherish, and I was thrilled to be able to announce to myself, "I want my life back, and I'm going to do everything possible to get it back." That was a pivotal moment in my decision to claim and pursue full health and recovery of my life: I wanted it back.

(Reflections after Sunday, May 7, 2000, day pass home before hospital discharge.)

Breaking Free: Negotiating My Way Beyond the Box

I desperately wanted to go home. At this point, nearly three weeks after my accident, I sensed I would receive no further benefit from remaining in the hospital rehab unit, and I wanted to check out my feeling by being home.[1]

So I requested: "Please give me a Sunday afternoon pass. This will be a good test and learning experience for me. I can arrange to be accompanied at all times. I will be taken care of well, and this will give the rehab staff a break. Also, the timing will not interfere with my rehab schedule."

My rehab physician replied, "OK. You've persuaded me. I will write an order for you to go home, for six hours tomorrow afternoon." By now my rehab doc had become warm and friendly with me. He was listening to me. What a relief.

My friend Craig was staying with me at the hospital and available to help me for two weeks. I arranged for us to be alone in my home that Sunday afternoon. I was exhausted from my still wounded body and from the cascade of emotions triggered by returning home. It felt wonderful to pass out on my own familiar, comfortable bed for four hours. It also felt good and healing to have quiet privacy as well as to have lucid thinking now after having been in a drug-induced stupor. Home at last.

I did *not* want to return to the hospital rehab unit that Sunday evening, May 7, 2000. I wanted to stay home and knew that I was ready. After my pass, I felt certain that I had received all the benefits I could from the inpatient rehab unit.

I also knew, however, that it would be unwise to leave the hospital AMA (against medical advice), and I knew my opinion of my readiness to leave did not match the staff's. If I left AMA, it might negatively affect my health insurance's payment for further treatment related to my ski accident. Also, the neuropsychologist had threatened to report me to the Board of Psychology and hinder my return to work if I did not cooperate with hospital recommended limits and constraints.

But I was determined to leave the Bay Area hospital for inpatient rehabilitation as soon as possible, with a medical discharge order. I had gotten out of the cage (the Vail bed structure, which had felt like a zoo cage or prison to me) and off the narcotics; now I wanted and needed to get beyond the box of hospital confinement.

Escaping from this box meant more than going beyond stereotypic, noncreative approaches and solutions. It felt like escaping the final box, the coffin. If I accepted the neuropsychologist's view of me, as the rehab staff and some friends and colleagues had, I was dead to my former life. I knew that this was not necessary. I was coming alive, back to my full life.

I felt not seen for my whole, true self by most of the rehab staff. With the exception of a few nurses at the very end of my hospital stay, no rehab staff asked about my feelings, perceptions, needs, and wishes. I was in that brain injury grid that convinced the staff that they understood my issues and how I would do. My rapid changes were interpreted as confabulation and my expressions of frustration as disinhibition. Moreover, for someone who loves being outside, the boxed-in experience of being in the hospital did feel like a coffin. I was still physically, mentally, emotionally, and spiritually very much alive. And though I understood the need for initial constraints, I desperately longed for my freedom.

On Monday morning I said to the first nurse who came to my room, "I need to have a conference meeting with my rehab doctors and staff as soon as possible. I believe that most of them are here on Monday morning."

After the nurse checked into my request, I was pleased to be told, "Not everyone is here, but your doctors are and they agree to meet with you."

Four of us met in my room, and I shared my experience: "I was home on pass yesterday afternoon and it felt wonderful. When it was time to take my medication, I noticed that I'd been sent home with the wrong dose. I called the unit and spoke with a nurse who replied, 'You must be confused. You were given the right medicines.' So I clarified with more detail: 'Aren't I given two white capsules in the afternoon and one orange capsule in the evening? It's the afternoon, and I was given one orange capsule.' The nurse then said, 'Wait a minute, I'll check.' After this, the nurse came back to the phone, sounded embarrassed, and said, 'You are right. I don't know how that could have happened. Could you come now and pick up two white capsules?' I said, 'I'm really too tired and want to have all of my allotted time at home. Craig is with me and says he can return to the unit and trade the orange for two white capsules for me right now. Is that OK?' I was relieved to hear the nurse say, 'Yeah. We can do that.' So with Craig's help, I managed to get my correct medication dosage yesterday afternoon. I'm paying attention to my medical needs, and I feel ready to return home. I would really love to be discharged today. I will *not* stay beyond this Friday, May 12, at the latest, because of family needs, including my daughter's care. I personally don't feel any need to stay here now. I realize that you might feel the need to test me, in order to feel confident about my readiness to leave the rehab unit. I hope not, but if so, I'm prepared to meet your challenges."

The inpatient rehab unit had planned for me to stay until at least May 16, 2000, according to my medical records. My insurance paid well, and later as I reviewed my medical bills and insurance reimbursements, I marveled at this hospital's billing finesse compared to the Reno hospital's, which received relatively little insurance payment for my neurosurgery and stay in their Trauma ICU and medical units. I wondered if money helped influence the rehab unit's view that I needed more prolonged inpatient treatment or if that was only because of the brain injury grid.

Test me, they did. I got yet another battery of intelligence and neuropsychological tests. Exhausting. I was also asked to plan a menu, shop for groceries (by foot), and cook a meal.

I asked, "Why am I, a woman, required to shop and cook, whereas male patients are not?" My questioning this sexism was never directly answered.

I was told, "Planning this menu, shopping, and cooking require multiple complex skills. We want to see if you're up to this mentally and physically, to make certain that you're adept at self-care."

With my current focus on negotiating my way out of the hospital, I realized that I needed to comply now rather than to challenge them further, so I said, "OK." I developed a menu, walked to the neighborhood grocery store and shopped (with staff escort), then focused on the recipes and slowly cooked the menu. The food turned out quite well, and the staff seemed to enjoy it.

After this ordeal, obviously checking out my reality testing, the staff asked, "How do you think this whole planning and preparing food project went?"

I replied, "Although I usually love to cook, doing it now was harder and slower than ever before. I really had to concentrate. Why would I want to cook for myself now? I'm tired. I need to focus on my healing. I have family and friends to help me. I like to eat fresh fruits and vegetables. There are good restaurants and take-out food in Berkeley. I have different needs and interests now."

On May 10, 2000, I wrote in my hospital journal: *Tired at the end of a nonstop day. After my shopping and cooking ordeal, had a wonderful long visit with my rehab doctor. I like him more and more: a trained physiatrist. He removed my last stitch (yeah!) and is arranging some great ophthalmology referrals, really understands my concerns with my eye. He was interested in my headache feedback. … He is thrilled at my apparent patience and judgment about wanting to wait to drive. We discussed many details, and we are working together now. What a relief. He is seeing me, not just relating to me as a typical, stereotyped patient syndrome. He wrote a pass for me to go to Nicole's concert tomorrow evening. Hooray.*

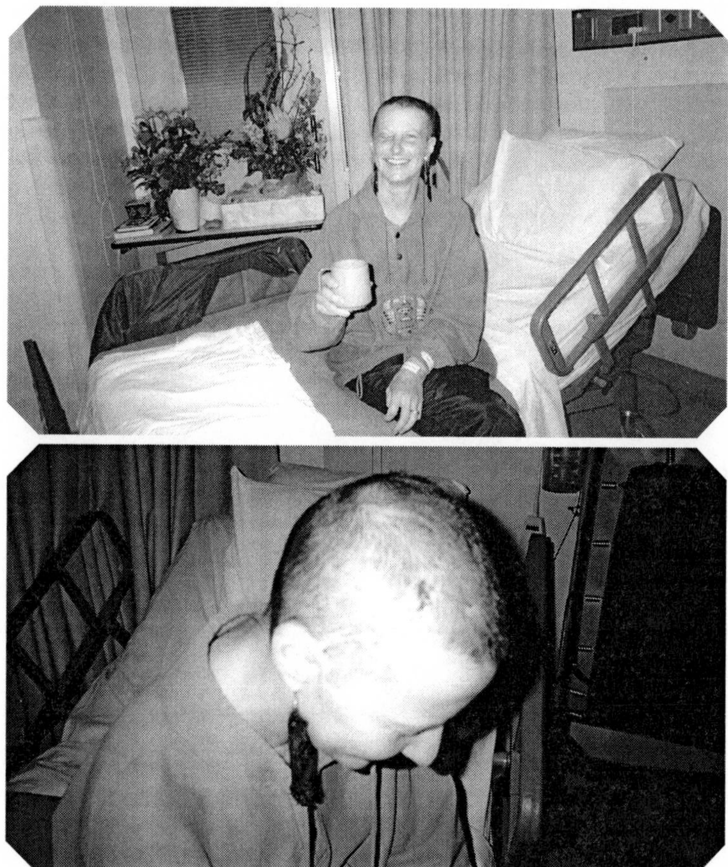

By rehab hospital bed just before discharge.

As the staff gradually accepted that I was ready for discharge, they helped me choose and have an initial assessment for outpatient rehab at home. I had discharge interviews with each medical discipline at the Bay Area hospital for inpatient rehabilitation, and I was released—with great joy—on Friday May 12, 2000, the day I had told the staff would be my latest acceptable discharge.

August 20, 2010

After going for my one-hour run as usual, still in my jogging clothes, I had stopped to buy fruits and vegetables. I was zipping around the store when suddenly before me, in a motorized shopping cart for people who have difficulty walking, there was a person I knew from graduate school in Berkeley in the 1970s. This person also happened to have been one of the staff neuropsychologists when I was at the Bay Area hospital for inpatient rehabilitation.

Surprised, I looked with concern and said "Hi. How are you?"

"You can see I've been better."

"I'm so sorry."

"I retired. Then three years ago, shortly before I had planned to travel, I was at home, got up in the dark at night, tripped, fell, broke my neck, and injured my head. I was paralyzed. Now after surgery and time to mend, I'm finally able to walk again and ready to take a trip to Europe."

"How scary and horrible that you had to go through all this, and after retirement. I recently thought of calling you at the hospital, not aware that you'd retired. It sounds like you've come a long way since that fall. You might still recover further; I hope so. I'm so glad you can travel now, and I hope you have a really good trip."

Then I was asked, "How are you? What are you up to these days?"

"You can see that I'm still running. I returned to my private practice and am still working. That's going well. I'm also writing a lot and really enjoying that."

I had not seen this grad school friend since May 2000 when I was given the following explanation at the Bay Area hospital for inpatient rehabilitation: "Your neuropsych testing showed a severe orbital frontal (brain) injury. You might never be able to work again as a psychologist." I was then given multiple examples of why and how my brain was not functioning properly. Now I was reconnected in person to the hospital rehabilitation experience, shortly after finishing the first draft of my book. This psychologist had tried to be kind and supportive to me, unlike the neuropsychologist assigned to my case. I had been grateful that this neuropsychologist was there at the hospital, with a gentle and smiling manner, though I had thought, *I disagree with your prognosis.*

This full circle of events reminded me of the powers of suggestion and expectation, as well as positive thinking and hope, in the process of healing. After any trauma, we have no idea how a person's healing will go: we are each unique in our healing. I was again reminded of how important it is to be related to in a kind manner, to feel listened to and supported, to be helped to expand on what is working well, and helped to creatively work around and cope with what is not working well.

Emotions? Inner landscape?

You've got to be kidding? Why would I focus on that? I'm in survival mode.

Being a climber and skier, "landscape" conjures images of the Himalayas as I tune inside to the experience of my ski accident. Two continents crashing into one another. Total chaos. A mess. Confusion. What will survive? How will it all re-form? What will the new shapes be like? Landscape that didn't exist before, lower and higher than ever before. I see the silhouette of majestic snow-capped peaks off in the distance. So far away. Unbelievably hard to get to.

First I need to dig my body out of the rubble. I need to rest.

How can I possibly get there? One step at a time? Or do I have to crawl? Slowly inching? I feel overwhelmed to even contemplate this.

(Reflection after spiritual director and psychologist friends asked me about my emotions, my "inner landscape.")

8

Inner Landscape

I found myself in a double bind while at the Bay Area hospital for inpatient rehabilitation, in an impossible situation that I could not directly and clearly address. A double bind is a psychological impasse that is created by a person in a position of power so that contradictory or conflicting demands are made: obeying one demand is to disobey the other. This creates a no-win communication situation which results in experiencing that whatever decision you make, you are wrong. For instance, if I went along with the neuropsychologist's view of my brain functioning, I would be giving up and accepting less than optimal recovery—not really trying my best—in a rehab unit ostensibly designed to help people recover after brain trauma; and if I went against the neuropsychologist's view of my brain functioning, I would be a difficult patient, unable to cooperate, ostensibly caused by and proof of my brain injury.

This double bind occurred partially because of the classic rehab view of what behavior is expected after severe brain injury. My recovering quickly did not fit into the usual brain injury grid. Some nursing staff, who spent the most time with me as nurses often do, did see how fast I was recovering and mostly did come alongside me and listen to me, as did my rehab physician toward the end of my hospitalization. Each time this attunement happened, I felt huge relief.

My EMT trained brother Jim later explained that even in the first five days—when I was in the trauma ICU—my "functioning far surpassed reasonable expectations and hope of expected functioning, given the severity" of my accident. Jim had expected me to die, at best to be only partially functional, yet he saw before leaving Reno on April 22, 2000, that I was beginning to come back, returning to my former self, and quickly. This matched what my neurosurgeon had seen during surgery, written in my hospital chart, and told my family.

The neuropsychologist assigned to me in the Bay Area hospital for inpatient rehabilitation called staff meetings with my family, friends, and professional colleagues, providing a hopeless, negative, suspicious view of my brain status and expected future functioning. I was not invited to these meetings and heard about them later from psychologist friends.

My friends were uncomfortable with the very negative prognosis, given by an expert, which did not match my visible improvements. I later heard from several: "This was very confusing for me. I felt stuck in the middle between being your friend and being your professional colleague during this time of crisis."

The neuropsychologist was convinced that I could not properly or adequately assess my own limitations and functioning. His focus was aimed at helping me remember and accept my deficits, difficulties, errors, and frustrations.

The neuropsychologist believed that I had to be reined in and carefully watched, to protect me as well as those affected by me. "If you return to your psychology practice in less than six months, you will be reported to the Board of Psychology and your license to practice might be revoked." That was a scary threat.

I was told: "Without being able to practice psychology, your sense of self will be deeply shaken, and you probably will be devastated emotionally."

I felt incensed at that proclamation and quietly thought to

myself: *Did anyone ask me? Nooooooo. There's a lot more to me than just my profession. Perhaps I would not only practice my piano more but could also learn to play the harp and saxophone, two instruments I really love. Perhaps I would take painting lessons or return to throwing pottery and writing poetry. At least I could go on long walks, probably hike again, and I know I would enjoy the beauty of nature. I love my work, and I have a huge life beyond being a psychologist. You've got no idea what makes me tick, and you've never asked.*

Yet, these challenges and depictions of me also resulted in my having doubts: *Was the neuropsychologist correct and I out of my mind? I've been fighting for my life and am still being told "no." Might I never be able to enjoy any aspects of my life again?*

But then I remembered: *Friends can already bring me to laughter with funny stories.*

With all of these questions and concerns, I felt confused and terrified. I particularly worried about Nicole, and my clients.

However, I gradually realized and was relieved to remember that I had more than just good oxygenated blood circulation and an athletic body, which helped me physically to survive this accident. I also had more than ten years of deep, personal psychotherapy during and after my PhD training, plus couple's therapy and different group therapies. I understood my family of origin issues well, had come to know my real (rather than false and adapted) self, and I had developed easy access to my emotions. In addition, I had years of development of close relationships and meaningful work, fun extracurricular interests and adventures, as well as spiritual practice, faith, and learning from many different spiritual retreats. All this inner work and life experience had combined to give me an integrated psyche.

My physical health plus inner work provided adequate brain functioning despite the severity of my accident. *And* I was very fortunate to receive the help I needed when I desperately needed it, every step along the way, beginning with first aid in the tree well and skilled neurosurgery.

Initially I was stuck in the hospital. There I had struggled to re-find some sense of my physical strength and to remember what had happened to me.

I worried about never feeling relaxed and without pain again, then about my memory and brain not functioning at its prior level, then about all I could not do. I experienced relative weakness and imbalance in my body and mind. I was sad about the many people who were negatively impacted by my accident. I was sad about missing our special vacation in Paris, and I was most particularly concerned about Nicole. When she visited me in the hospital, I could see fear and sadness in her eyes. I also worried and prayed for my clients, particularly a few who had been in crisis as well as those who had been doing deep psychotherapeutic work with me. I worried about how I would survive financially, as a self-employed single parent, without working. I was sad about my loss of attractiveness: I looked older and quite scary after hitting that tree. I used to look young for my age; no longer. I was in grief about my relationship disappointments and the rapid health decline of my aging parents. I was angry and sad about not being seen for my real and full self by some of the rehab staff. I felt discontent about how I and some other patients were treated in the rehab unit. My body, mind, emotions, and spirit all felt highly anxious, stuck in a fight or flight response, with much less tolerance of both small and big challenges than before my accident. I cried easily. I missed and longed for freedom.

I was also very happy to be alive and to be healing relatively rapidly. I so appreciated feeling loved and supported by those close to me. I felt the power of being prayed for by many people. I enjoyed having time to sleep and rest for many hours, which was an unusual experience for me, but forced by my down-to-the-bones exhaustion. I received food, visits, and stories that made me laugh, plus loving touch, with much gratitude. In all these ways, I felt deeply blessed.

I felt everything more intensely and in different ways than ever before.[1, 2] I learned in time that this often happens to people who have survived a big trauma, that the attendant unusually intense negative and positive emotions are often experienced as confusing and sometimes as overwhelming. I learned that complementary/alternative/integrative therapies, including body therapies, could help with sorting through strong emotions and supporting healing. I experienced a deep and slow settling and resetting of my body-mind-emotions-spirit. I later came to understand, after training in somatic therapy, that it is easy to confuse the effects of brain injury, narcotic medications, and trauma response; the distinction here is important because each requires a different treatment approach.[3]

In July, three months after my accident, my trauma fight or flight On switch reset itself during a craniosacral body therapy session (more about this in Chapter 14). Then I was finally able to think more clearly so that I could solve multiple problems created by my accident, one step at a time, without being incapacitated by anxiety. In fact, I felt some emotional relief each time I received complementary/alternative help, which began with Joan's massages in the hospital. This was interesting, because my main motivation for seeking complementary/alternative/holistic help had been to heal my aching body and the injured cranial nerves connected to my right eye. I was far more drawn to body therapies than to talking psychotherapy at this time in my life, a new experience for me.[4] This integrative healing process eventually provided me with a broader and deeper inner landscape, an expansion of my professional work, and a more palpable trust in life and death.[5]

A good, productive, yet painful and very tough day. I spent the morning doing household chores, while Dave[1] *worked away accomplishing the rest of my to-do list, bless his heart. Kelley, Dave, and I also worked together to reorganize the deck furniture and two of the bedrooms, also to cook the meals. Exhausting. After my acupuncture appointment, which lasted more than two hours, I felt totally spent. Meanwhile, Kelley and Dave had taken Nicole to Adventure Playground for two hours, and fortunately they all had a blast. Back home, we quickly had dinner and then were off to Nicole's music concert. When we all got home late, at the end of this nonstop day, all I wanted to do was crash, but first I needed to do exercises for my jaw (I'm doing them three times a day and it is improving!) and take my pills. I apologized to everyone for being so on edge and explained that I was trying to get going as quickly as possible after the concert. I'm noticing that the longer this recovery process lasts, the harder it feels. The pain is wearing on me. I have less tolerance than usual for Nicole's childlike behaviors when she challenges me, especially when I'm tired. The novelty of what happened, of having survived, and the joy of getting out of that bloody hospital are all less potent. I want to be well – and sooner than later!*

(Excerpt from my journal, written eight days after I got out of the hospital, before I learned the arts of patience and moving at a more gentle rhythm.)

9

One Step at a Time: Coping with Many Mini-Traumas

It was a relief to be home again. But this was far from the end of my post-accident journey. Fortunately, I had family or friends staying with me the first month back home. My health insurance did eventually cover most of my accident and rehab bills. Rehab Without Walls did outpatient rehab and worked skillfully with me. I got to return to my trusted medical and complementary/alternative/integrative medicine professionals, as well as find new, needed specialists. Friends and family helped me care for Nicole.

Perseverance is a strong aspect of my personality. Patience is something I was painfully forced to learn. Recovery and full healing became a major, more than half time occupation for many months, and I did have some savings that helped cover expenses.

After a serious accident or illness, it is common to have many unexpected problems in addition to the medical issues. I have seen this with others in my work and with friends and family. Now I experienced it myself.

Understanding and coping with a complex medical problem can seem almost equivalent to getting a university degree. For instance, I had to study eye functioning and healing, as well as find specialists, in order to get my right eye open again (details about that in Chapter 11). But I found that sleep, fresh air, feeling loved, laughter, prayer, enlisting help, having separate interests that provided positive distraction and respite, plus tackling things one at a time helped me cope.

Too many mini-traumas along with a big trauma felt overwhelming. As I write now, over a decade after my big ski accident, the list of all I had to do seems daunting still. It was naturally much harder to sort through back then, because of my mental and physical fatigue. But because I had many sources of help and because I really could attend to recovery only one step at a time, I kept doing just that.

Being a mountain climber, I understood deep in my bones that even a huge mountain is literally climbed one small step at a time. It is my hope that all doctors, healthcare providers, family members, friends, patients, and clients will remember the values of patience and perseverance: mountains, recovery, health, and life are all done one step at a time.

For this post-accident time of many mini-traumas, I needed to:

- Seek detailed medical help for my still unresolved physical problems.
- Help my daughter who was obviously hurting.
- Improve my healing through PT and exercise.
- Cope with financial demands including hospital bills and insurance payments, household needs and expenses.
- Return to work as quickly as possible, as well as possible.
- Navigate transportation to multiple appointments (especially difficult while not driving).
- Navigate and cope with complex, coincidental yet unrelated needs of extended family and friends.

A few examples of coincidental mini-traumas were situations in my home, with my parents, and with friends. Three specific examples are shared here.

Because of increased bills and no income, financial pressures were mounting. I needed to change the configuration of my house, sectioning off the back one third to form an apartment.

"I know I need to get an apartment set up in the back of my house, but I'm too exhausted and broke to be able to plan or pay for this construction," I told my brother Dave who was staying with me to help after my hospital discharge.

"Craig is here, and I bet that he and I can engineer a soundproof system of walls within two days, so you can rent out this space as an apartment, to help your mortgage payments," Dave replied.

"That would be fantastic, if you could do this."

"No problem," Craig chimed in.

"It would be more than a problem for me to try to do this myself," I said, as I watched them skillfully construct and paint three removable double soundproof walls.

As I watched them work away quickly, I felt gratitude. But then I felt overwhelmed about needing to find a renter.

Fortunately, my friend Maryann visited that day. She asked, "How are you doing?"

"I need to find a renter and do all the related paperwork and logistics, but my brain is too exhausted to even think about how to do this."

"I can easily do this for you. I have all the information you need to secure a good renter: where to list your rental, credit check information, an application form, deposit form, and a rock solid lease I drafted and passed by an attorney for approval," Maryann responded immediately. She could see my quizzical look and added, "I put this all together when we had a renter, and I have it in a file at home. I'll bring it to you tomorrow."

The next day, Maryann did bring and explain the paperwork and process I needed to secure a good renter.

The help of Dave, Craig, and Maryann was a financial boost

that has continued on a monthly basis. Within a week, I had a nice renter in place.

My stepdad Severt died of old age three months before my accident. He and I had been co-executors for my mom who at that time was institutionalized with end-stage Alzheimer's. He chose to manage everything, since they were in Oregon and I was in California.

Severt's death left me as sole guardian and executor for my mom. All the financial and executor paperwork arrived about the same time I got home from the rehab unit. I could not make heads or tails of it.

I had always been gifted at math, yet I was unable to understand the numbers in the stacks of papers, even with focused concentration and a calculator. I thought to myself: *Maybe I really am a goner. No matter how I manipulate these numbers, it does not make sense to me.*

After a few days of unsuccessful effort, I decided to contact the Elder Law Attorney[2] in Eugene, Oregon, chosen by my mom and stepdad. Though this felt scary, I shared with her by phone: "Helen, I've spent hours and hours going over all of the financials and paperwork for my parents, and I can't make sense of it. I was in a bad accident and had a head injury. Maybe I'm not mentally competent to actually be my mom's executor now that Severt has died."

"If you want, mail it to me, and I'll look at it for you," Helen offered.

"Yes. Wonderful," I replied.

Helen called me back a few weeks later and explained, "Carole, your confusion was not due to your head injury. All the paperwork was in horrible disarray, probably because Severt had not been able to attend to it during his last year of life. I'd be happy to sort this out and then turn it over to you."

"What a relief to hear this from you, Helen. Yes, please help me."

"You can always call me if you need further help in the future, after I return and explain this paperwork to you."

"Thank you so much for all your help for my parents."

After receiving Helen's organized paperwork and then discussing it by phone, I was able to take on the financial and medical overseeing of care for my mom, until she died two years later. I also was able to keep my brothers and stepsister updated, and I visited my mom as often as possible. I thankfully was able to be at Mom's side as she died.

My friend Margaret[3] got cancer four months after my accident, and I was her durable power of attorney for healthcare. Margaret had no children and was single at that time. I naturally wanted to help her, as she had helped me.

"Why don't you come stay in my home, after your cancer surgery and hospitalization?" I offered without hesitation.

"But where would I stay?" Margaret asked.

"In my bedroom, the room with the view," was my immediate reply. "I know it's still a bit of a disaster after the reconfiguration of the house, plus my not being able to keep up with everything since my accident and hospitalization. But I think I'm feeling well enough to organize the space for you now, and I can stay in the guest room."

"Are you sure?"

"Absolutely." Then to be clear, I added: "You know, I need to work, take care of Nicole, and I'm still seeing many doctors. I can pick you up from the hospital and bring you home. I'll do all I can to help you and make you comfortable, but I can't be present 24/7."

"Other friends can take shifts bringing me food and visiting with me. Besides, I need time to myself and will need time to rest, sleep, and heal," Margaret said.

Margaret and I were both shocked and scared by the proximity of her cancer to my accident. She stayed in my home after her first cancer surgery and hospitalization, and I tried to help her, though this was really too soon after my own hospital discharge. I did not have as much time as I wanted to devote to Margaret because I was still trying to recover from my accident.

My life was complex before the accident. Now it was even more complex at a time when I needed to rest and heal. One problem was followed by another. But slowly I was able to sort through these problems and get all the medical and logistical help needed so that I could heal, get on with my life, and be supportive to others.

I walked Nicole to school this morning because I can't drive. "Please wear a scarf, Mommy. You look scary and I don't want the other kids at school to make fun of me."

"OK," and we chatted as we enjoyed being able to walk together.

Then two blocks from school, Nicole said, "Please walk behind me now, Mommy," as she told me to move back three paces. 'Oh my.' I thought, while I moved as directed.

Then I noticed that everyone we passed was staring at me. So I started paying attention to how people in numerous locations are reacting to me: looking and relating with horror, pity, awkwardness, discomfort, fear. Some comments are made, based on what they experience internally. Hardly anyone asks me how I am or if I need help. Hardly anyone wants to really talk with me at all, unless we already have a relationship, and sometimes not even then. Most people react to my appearance; it's as if I don't exist beyond whatever is triggered in them. The whole me is not seen.

Ouch. Then I realize that many people in the world must experience this all the time: discomfort with others because of "differences." Sad.

I look more than a bit different.

(Excerpt from my journal, three days after I got out of the hospital.)

10

Beyond Limitations, Broken Mirrors

One important insight I took away from my ski accident is the problem of "broken mirrors," of not being clearly seen, which often occurs after a big trauma.[1] One person's trauma can result in painful reverberations to many—including family, friends, helping professionals, people connected to our work, even passersby. What gets reflected back can be a combination of the other's own trauma experiences and perceptions, secondary trauma evoked by seeing the injured person, and personal fears, thereby not seeing traumatized persons for who and how they really are in the moment. This is made worse when a traumatized person looks scary or odd, as I did.

I learned how important it is to tune inside—to look from the inside out—and to get help doing this whenever needed. Being a psychologist, I know from experience as receiver and as therapist that a good psychotherapist can be helpful in this way. Emotionally open, intimate others who know how to listen and reflect well can be essential. This might include a family member, friend, or other helping professional.

During an exit interview from the Bay Area hospital for inpatient rehabilitation, my assigned neuropsychologist announced, "We've gone over all your test results. Your biggest problem is your brain…."

Because my main aim at that time was to get out of the hospital, I refrained from saying what I really thought and felt: *You don't have a clue about me. All you know is your tests and scoring, along with your rigid idea of what should be going on after the accident I had. If you actually paid attention to my meds and progress, you would see that my brain was not as damaged as you believe it must be. I'm pleased with how much better I am already, and so quickly. You have no idea how much I'm restraining myself from saying what I think and feel about you right now. I do understand that I could not control myself emotionally if my brain were not working. Yes, my tests are not what they would have been before my accident. But they are still well above average, and I'm still on the mend. So bugger off. Thank God I'm leaving this joint.*

Instead, I "appropriately" said, "I know my brain needs to heal over time, and right now I'm more concerned about my closed right eye and visual problems."

I disagreed with the neuropsychologist's perception. It was astonishing to me to be told in detail about my problems and *never* asked about my concerns.

Later in the summer of 2000, while reading my Reno medical records, I was surprised and affirmed to learn that the neurosurgeon and trauma doctor were concerned about my right eye and related visual difficulties: *Patient has significant swelling and bruising of the right eyelid, cheek, orbital area, and scalp, …sluggish dilated pupil on the right possibly from direct trauma* (written the day of my accident). *…findings could be consistent with orbital fracture* (written after ophthalmology consultation five days later). *She needs evaluation by a neuro-ophthalmologist….* (written a day later when transferred out of ICU). They saw my right eye damage clearly during my initial evaluation and surgery on April 16, 2000 (but more about healing my vision in Chapter 11).

Excerpt from my journal: July 18, 2000: … *During a follow-up appointment, Dr. Litwin*[2] (who is still—in 2015— my general ophthalmologist) *explained to me: "I could hardly stand to look at you the first time you came to see me—such a young and alive person, so hurt. It was both easy and hard to identify with. I imagine the hospital staff had a hard time seeing you for your whole self. All they could see was your head injury. You were one of us—bright, vibrant, a healthcare provider. And then suddenly it looked like you were snuffed out. Your situation was too close to home—this was intolerable. It could happen to any of us. And you were no longer seen."*

I replied: "Thank you for being so open with me. You are my eye doctor, and you were the first doctor in the Bay Area to actually see me for who I still am when I had my initial appointment in your office." I finally understood more clearly a part of why I had been treated in ways that felt disturbing to me.

"Why don't you read Ram Dass's 'Still Here'[3]—his newest book, about whole presence, even after his stroke. I know him, and his book is quite amazing," said Dr. Litwin. He then hugged me goodbye, and said, "You're a great person." Wow! What a surprise.

I purchased Ram Dass's book as soon as I could.

The broken mirrors happened in many areas of my life, in subtle and not so subtle ways. In each case, whether with healthcare providers, family members, friends, colleagues, people involved in big systems, even strangers, I had to:

- Be patient so I could tune inside my body for my inner truth in order to
- Seek more helpful, clarifying feedback, and information so I could
- Discern multiple complex, shifting concerns plus interrelated problems, and
- Gradually come to know the steps toward greatest healing for me through solutions that could help me
- Move beyond initial limitations, including those limitations imposed on me by others as well as those felt inside during my healing journey.

By tuning in to your own body and evoking your own self-image, you can see whether the mirror of yourself as given by others feels true or broken, then notice limitations that might be unnecessary if you patiently work toward your fullest healing. I learned after my big accident that body therapies and somatic psychotherapies[4] are particularly helpful in learning how to tune inside my body for feedback that enables me to feel specific changes—sensations, emotions, and thoughts. From this feedback I can more clearly discern what support is still needed to facilitate further healing (more details in Chapter 16).

At home a month after hospital discharge.

Scar on right head and face.

Another fabulous day of fresh powder skiing in Taos; here for my annual birthday ski trip. Time to play with family and friends, feeling very loved—great ski lesson with Jean,[1] *hot tub with the girls, massage, delectable French food. I'm so glad to be alive still, able to enjoy every detail.*

Dinner was yummy and a riot—we all dressed in costume for Mardi Gras. We were seated at a table for ten, including four very nice doctors on their 20th annual ski trip together. Sitting across from me was Martyn,[2] *an ophthalmologist, who, thankfully, was very observant.*

"What happened to your eye?" he asked.

I told him my story.

"Do you mind if I check out your eye movements?"

"Please do."

"The problem was caused by a crushed orbital floor, blocking muscle movement," he said. "It isn't just a crushed nerve. Although the shattered bone should have been fixed surgically two to three weeks after the accident, it may be repairable still." Martyn thought that my strabismus doctor had lost sight of the big picture of the injury, and he offered to find the most highly skilled oculoplastic surgeon in the country.

"I want my eye to be healed, and I'm willing to go anywhere," I replied to his generous offer.

I was grateful for this chance meeting at a dinner table in Taos Ski Valley, which proved more informative and hopeful than the past nine months of seeking eye doctors back home.

(Excerpt from my journal, written February 27, 2001, two days before my 49th birthday.)

Shifting My View

I wrote the first draft of this book from memory, by hand, while sitting in a rocking chair looking either at the view from my home of the city of San Francisco with the Golden Gate Bridge or the view from my cabin of the woods and South Upper Truckee River within the Eldorado National Forest near Lake Tahoe. I had to write from this embodied, hands on, visual way, for reasons unclear to me then. I wrote in a stream of consciousness, without fact checking or worrying about correct grammar.

Later when I began editing my book, I saw how my right eye saga spread through many chapters and was as confusing as the experience itself: hard to follow, like a huge, complicated labyrinth. So I decided to give my right eye healing its own chapter. It was cumbersome to lift this story out of the entire book and tell it in a clear way—very much a mirror of my eye healing experience.

Immediately after the accident everyone could see that my right eye was swollen and closed, plus I had two black eyes from the force of hitting that tree. Nevertheless, my right eye problem was forgotten about entirely at the Bay Area hospital for inpatient rehabilitation until Craig reminded my rehab doctor.

"Carole had fractures in the floor and lateral wall of her right eye orbit. Her Reno doctors believed this needs follow-up as soon as possible. I think you will find this in her hospital record from Washoe Medical Center," said Craig.

"I will look into this," responded my rehab doctor.

Then while still an inpatient, I was sent to an ophthalmologist (eye doctor), Richard L. Litwin,[3] whose office is near my home. This was my first time ever to see an ophthalmologist outside a hospital because I do not wear glasses and had no eye problems before my accident.

Dr. Litwin examined me carefully and said, "Your left eye is functioning well, and you need to see specialists for your closed right eye after discharge from the hospital to see if your optic (eye) nerve still functions for your right eye and, if so, what can be done about opening your right eyelid and about getting your right eye muscles to function as well as possible. But you will need to allow time for your eye to heal naturally before having any ophthalmic surgeries. If surgery is done too soon, your eye would continue to heal and then a different problem would be created: you might need subsequent surgery to correct the first surgery. Patience, patience."

Patience with myself was not my forte. But my right eye forced me to learn patience in a new way.

My closed right eye and resultant visual, and therefore balance, problems were my greatest physical concerns when I was discharged from the hospital 27 days after my ski accident. This did not match the concern of my rehab hospital neuropsychologist: my brain. It was fortunate that my brain worked relatively well, because I had to deal with the complexities of my eye and other health problems post-hospitalization.

During a six-year eye-healing journey I saw more than a dozen eye doctors and had three eye surgeries. As part of this, I did many alternative therapies to get my right eyelid to open, then to stop having kaleidoscopic vision, and finally to decrease my double vision as much as possible. I learned a tremendous amount about how eyes work and about different surgical specialties of eye doctors.

If you are interested in eyes, their functioning and healing, I invite you to read some details of my experience in the rest of this chapter. I particularly wrote this detailed eye healing chapter to illustrate the power of Integrative Medicine: the concomitant use of Western/allopathic medicine and surgery along with Eastern/alternative/complementary treatments that together result in holistic medicine, to optimally provide maximal healing.[4]

The first ophthalmologist I saw after inpatient discharge was a specialist in oculofacial plastic, reconstructive, and orbital surgery, because of the concern about my right eye orbit: perhaps the nerves or muscles were entrapped in the fractures. This surgeon explained, "You have third nerve palsy (paralysis) and partial seventh nerve palsy; these cause your right eyelid to be entirely closed and your right eye muscles to be only partially functioning. There is no evidence of blowout fracture nerve or muscle entrapment. These nerves were apparently crushed. They might never regenerate."

"Isn't there some surgery that could help my right eyelid open and be more normal?"

"None that I know of. You should wait for up to a year to see if you get some spontaneous healing." Seeing the displeasure in my face, this doctor added, "I know of no surgery that will get an entirely closed eyelid to open. I guess you could call UCSF[5] and see if there is some new experimental surgery. If the lid does not open, the eye muscles are irrelevant. Though you are able to see when your lid is held open by hand, you might never have functional use of that eye again."

This news felt upsetting and depressing to me, because not having use of two eyes created a problem with depth perception and with seeing on the right side of my body. I also looked pretty weird, though I tried not to focus on my appearance.

Next I saw a neuro-ophthalmologist in San Francisco, Richard K. Imes.[6] His examination revealed: "Your right eye is neurologically intact. There is no problem with the optic (eye) nerve itself; and you have normal optic disc, vessels, and macula. The right lid just will not open, and the right eye muscles are only partially working. You did crush cranial nerves III and VII."

But, by holding my right eyelid up, Dr. Imes found: "Your vision in both eyes and your pupils' reactivity to light are functioning well now. Your right eye is already functioning better today (May 30, 2000) than it did in Reno in April. This improved pupillary function is a good sign that predicts at least some recovery from your other eye problems."

"Thank you for examining me so carefully, for giving me hope for further healing."

I was already hearing conflicting opinions from eye experts: The orbital fractures were a problem and needed surgical attention (Reno hospital ophthalmologist), then they did not (first oculoplastic surgeon I saw); I had crushed cranial nerves III and VII, but one said III and IV (a general ophthalmologist, which was incorrect); the only hope of using my right eye again was if I had spontaneous healing, but given the severity of my injury that was unlikely, then my now improved pupillary function was a good predictive sign of at least some more recovery.

As Dr. Remen wisely wrote: "The power of the expert is very great and the way in which an expert sees you may easily become the way in which you see yourself."[7] I had coped with a pessimistic view of my brain recovery by the rehab staff, and now I was coping with contradictory feedback from eye experts.

While recently reviewing all my eye records for accuracy of memory, I saw that the tone and style of communication by an expert also have huge emotional impact. For instance, I heard total pessimism about the healing of my right eyelid when a doctor expressed no hope, and I felt better after a doctor expressed some potential hope. In my brain this got translated to believing that one doctor thought my right eyelid would never open and one thought it probably would, whereas the recorded notes by these doctors regarding their examinations of me were very similar. From all of this, I have come to a broader understanding of the power of how we see another and, also, how we communicate what we see.

Right eye closed before beginning alternative treatments.

It was time for a vacation, and my family with friends went to our cabin in the mountains. My right eyelid first opened during this time of relaxation, even though only a tiny bit. What a surprise.

After our vacation, I returned to my ptosis (oculoplastic/eyelid) doctor and I saw a strabismus (eye muscle) specialist, to get input about what I could do to help my lid open further and my eye muscles move more normally—to help my crushed cranial nerves heal. I was told by both doctors, "You might spontaneously heal a bit more. Eyes are complicated and unique, because they work in tandem. I know of nothing to help nerves as crushed as yours to heal. You probably will not have normal use of your otherwise functional right eye. If the nerves do spontaneously heal more, they will only regenerate for six to twelve months." As it turned out, mine continued regenerating for more than five years.

I asked, "Is there any problem if I try acupuncture or other alternative healing approaches?"

"You're a psychologist. You know even better than I do that what we believe is important. It won't hurt you. If you want to, give it a try."

I learned from my eye-healing saga that we healthcare providers need to believe in the healing potential of our patients. We need to ask them what they believe, what they want to try, and then encourage them. In 1983, I had written a paper on hope, based on my dissertation research: a sense of hope was the strongest single variable in positive recovery from grief.[8] I was studying grief after divorce and bereavement, not hope. But hope emerged as very important in the data analysis.

The prediction of probable non-healing, though my eyelid had opened a bit in two and a half months, caused me to seek hopeful and helpful eye doctors. I also sought every kind of alternative/complementary healing that might help my cranial nerves regenerate.

I was on a focused mission: to have use of my right eye again. All of this took a lot of time (six years) and money. I had more nerve regeneration than even my excellent eye surgeons ever imagined possible, though the nerve regeneration was aberrant, required some surgical help, and continued for a year after my third eye surgery.

I live in Berkeley, in the Bay Area in Northern California, which has many alternative health practices. I had already been receiving massage therapy regularly, plus physical therapy and acupuncture as needed, before my ski accident. I had experienced the power and unique helpfulness of hands-on healing techniques and Eastern Medicine. So right after discharge from the hospital, I returned to my acupuncturist, Lynn Segura[9] in Berkeley, for twice a week sessions initially, to help my overall healing and energy level after such a traumatic accident. To help my eye heal, Lynn added specific eye points to her comprehensive healing regime for me; she also added electrical stimulation through needles around my right eye. That was not fun, especially a few times when the machine accidentally sent electric bursts to these needles. I dubbed this "Chinese torture" and coped by joking about it with Lynn so we laughed together, but I noticed it helped my eyelid open a bit more, which gave me the courage to endure the occasional shocking pain. Acupuncture also, along with much rest and sleep, helped my kaleidoscopic vision—which had emerged with the first opening of my eyelid—shift to double vision, a true relief.

I saw Greg Schelkun,[10] in San Rafael, a Filipino trained hands-on spiritual healer, recommended by a psychologist friend for help in healing my cranial nerves. Greg had an encouraging, healing presence. He has received recognition for his alternative treatments, particularly with cancer patients. I did not notice that Greg helped my right eye specifically, and that was my aim. However, seeing Greg did help me to accept my hospital experiences in a new way, to be grateful for my survival and current healing path in a deeper way. Other alternative treatments I tried included specialized therapeutic eye massage and neuromuscular massage therapy with an emphasis on the eye. I tried all recommended treatments that might help my right eye heal, and I could tell fairly quickly whether these approaches yielded visible results.

Friends as well as clients recommended that I try CranioSacral therapy (CST)[11] to help my right eye. I located two masters: first Cathy Adachi[12] in the East Bay, until she moved to Chicago (August 2001); then Katrina Auer,[13] a CST and shamanistically trained healer in San Rafael, until she moved to North Carolina (August 2003). The CST, though subtle and gentle, was the strongest single alternative healing method that facilitated the opening of my right eyelid. For instance, I saw Katrina beginning August 2001, and after each hour-long session of CST with her, my right eyelid was open wider. Katrina first relaxed my occipital (back of the head) muscles with deep massage, which felt so good to my aching head and neck. Then her work focused on normalizing my sphenoid, the butterfly shaped bones that hold the eyes, through which the cranial nerves that innervate the eyelid and muscles must past. This part of my skull was quite fractured after crashing into the tree.

Although the visual stress of driving from San Rafael caused my eyelid to be a little less open by the time I got back to Berkeley, it was stunning to observe my lid opened wider than ever since my accident by the end of each CST session. I started looking in the bathroom mirror at the end of each session, then again when back at my Berkeley office, to monitor how my right eye was doing. Until I saw Katrina, I had avoided looking in the mirror more than once a day after my accident. Now I could see the impact of how my eye was connected to my sphenoid was connected to my neck was connected to my double vision. I had to tilt my neck back a bit to have singular vision for driving; my downgaze was my only normal stereoscopic vision—intact/singular and not double—due to injured eye muscles. Tilting my head back to help my vision not only hurt my neck a bit (probably because of my C-6-7 fractures), it also hurt my sphenoid bone structure and cerebral spinal fluid rhythm in the dural tube, which resulted in my eyelid closing a little each time I drove. But very gradually, my right eye opened more and more, thanks in particular to CST and acupuncture.

While I was working with these complementary treatments, I

was referred (via Martyn, whom I met in Taos) to Stuart R. Seiff,[14] in San Francisco, an eye surgeon and specialist in orbital (bone), eyelid, and lacrimal (tear duct) surgeries. I had discussed my right eye orbit problem with each of my ophthalmologists in the Bay Area, but it was either not their specialty or not seen as an issue before I met Dr. Seiff, May 7, 2001.

"I am really upset about the damage caused by the delay of my needed eye orbit repair. This is my first eye surgery, and it should have been done within the first month after my accident," I said as I discussed my eyes with Dr. Seiff.

"You had so many other more critical issues, this one got missed. We will attend to this now," Dr. Seiff replied, as he quickly thumbed through my thick medical record and then looked at my x rays from Reno.

The first three weeks after my accident, there were other more critical issues. By the fourth week, when I was busy negotiating and proving my capacity for release from the inpatient rehab unit, I could and should have had the blowout fracture surgery, from what I now understand, I thought but did not say.

Dr. Seiff examined me carefully, ordered a CT scan, and did not waste time. On May 16, 2001, exactly 13 months after my accident, Dr. Seiff surgically repaired my right blowout fracture.

After surgery, Dr. Seiff explained: "I did a right orbital fracture repair that included release of entrapped tissue stuck in your broken lower orbit, what I had seen on the CT scan. This increased your capacity for upgaze; your right eye is no longer stuck so badly in downgaze. Now your right eye can relearn to look up, just as your eyelid already relearned to open, because both of these muscles—superior rectus and levator—run off the same branch of the 3rd cranial nerve that was crushed by your accident."

My nerves were still regenerating. After the right blowout fracture surgery, I could see the difference between my primary vision image and the secondary double image. The secondary image changed, became more diffuse, and the primary image became stronger and clear by comparison. While driving to see Dr. Seiff for my first post-op follow-up, I noticed that my straight-ahead vision was more singular, without having to tilt my neck back so far to stop the double vision. Tilting to enable single vision had become a habit by then. So I played with looking straight ahead without tilting my neck until my double vision gradually fused into one image. Again and again I did this, retraining my eyes and brain while I sat in my office working and while I drove—unless I was too tired or the traffic too intense. What a relief for my brain, neck, and eyes!

I am grateful for Dr. Seiff. He saw the need for this surgery, even a year after my accident, quickly ordered current radiology images, then did the repair with skill and a kind, reassuring, no-nonsense attitude. Dr. Seiff joked after the surgery: "You can't expect to be good at shooting hoops now" (because my right eye upgaze was the least normal, still giving me double vision).

When I saw him later for a post-op appointment, I got to tease him right back: "I was visiting my nephews in Oregon. They invited me to shoot some hoops with them, and I sunk it in, the first shot." I said, as we both chuckled.

It was a surprise for me, yet understandable based on bone and nerve anatomy, to find after Dr. Seiff's blowout fracture repair that acupuncture and CST treatments helped my right eyelid open further and my eye muscles' movements improve more rapidly and fully than before his surgery.

Meir Schneider, an eye healer and teacher in San Francisco, helped himself heal from blindness to seeing, then developed a school and foundation to help others.[15] Beginning June 2002, I saw him for hands-on healing and to learn eye exercises specific for my problems.

I had asked my first three strabismus (eye muscle) doctors, "What kind of eye exercises would you recommend to help my muscles heal?"

"These can't help because eyes work in tandem and are very complicated," they claimed.

And what about neuromuscular training exercises? I know the power of repetitive exercises for improving physical functioning through training myself as an athlete along with my work as a sports psychologist. Aren't we talking about my eye nerves and muscles? I thought, but did not bother to ask.

The doctors thought "no." Meir thought "yes." I learned "yes" while I experimented, found helpful exercises, and practiced more singular vision after my blowout fracture repair.

I started doing Meir's eye exercises while running around a track. This tested and stretched my eye muscles while I moved in a safe venue. I not only still had double vision in my upgaze, I also had the effect of one eye moving with speed while the other eye acted as a still camera. This made me dizzy and threw off my balance at high speed. For instance, I still can no longer tolerate tucking while snow skiing. (My return to skiing, an important part of my rehab, is described in Chapter 20.) It was good to work with the eye exercises while running on a flat dirt track; at slow and moderate speeds, I saw very gradual improvement over time. For example, while jogging I shifted my vision from just in front of me to many feet ahead and then further ahead, then from left to right, back and forth in multiple directions, as I trained my eye muscles to move and my eyes to adjust while in motion. This double tasking—doing eye exercises while out running—also saved me time.

Meir and my strabismus (eye muscle) doctor both suggested, "Try wearing a patch over your good (left) eye occasionally, while running on a track now, and later while skiing on a beginner slope. This will force your injured right eye to work." I did it, though my body protested, with mild symptoms typical for anxiety and stress—more rapid breathing and pulse, along with fear.[16] I used the cognitive therapy technique of positive self-talk, to reassure my body: *You can do this, honey. The environment is safe. Enduring this challenge will help you heal.*

I know all these exercises helped, as well as the alternative medicine and hands-on treatments I received. My vision improved. I could see the difference in the reflection of my eyes in the mirror as well as by experiencing less double vision.

In 2001 and 2002, after Dr. Seiff's repair of my right eye orbit bones, I met with every strabismus (eye muscle) and ptosis (eyelid) surgeon in the greater Bay Area who was recommended to me. I was looking for the doctor(s) who best could help repair my right eye muscles and eyelid with surgery. This was a confusing and discouraging ordeal. Each of over a dozen doctors recommended a somewhat different surgery. I had hoped that two or three might suggest the same approach. One doctor even claimed he could fix the muscles and eyelid at the same time, though all the others were specialized in one or the other and said the eye orbit muscles should be repaired at least a month before the eyelid.

I gradually understood that it was wise to rule out specialists who mostly did surgery on children. I saw that their approach with me—and my eyes—was entirely different from those surgeons trained and skilled at helping adults with traumatic eye injuries.

In the end, I had to tune into myself to ascertain which surgeons I trusted the most. For the ptosis surgery, I decided to stay with Dr. Seiff. Then I chose Creig S. Hoyt[17] as my strabismus surgeon. I subsequently learned that he was Chair of the Ophthalmology Department at UCSF Medical School. Still later, I learned from Meir Schneider that Dr. Hoyt was world-renowned and had repaired Meir's son's eye muscles.

When I first met Dr. Hoyt, April 2002, he assumed that my spontaneous right eye nerve regeneration was complete and said, "I think by now the timing is good for us to prepare for your strabismus surgery."

"I'm not certain. I think my nerves may still be healing." I said, remembering what Dr. Litwin had explained to me about waiting for surgery as long as any eye nerve regeneration was continuing from inside the body, though I wanted to have surgery and be done with this.

"Really?" said Dr. Hoyt, aware through our conversation and my medical records that my first visit at the UCSF strabismus clinic was nearly two years after my ski accident and eleven months after Dr. Seiff's blowout fracture surgical repair. Dr. Seiff had told me to wait at least six months before pursuing strabismus surgery. So I used that time to search out more doctors until I met Dr. Hoyt.

Dr. Hoyt listened carefully and responded, "Well then, let me measure your eye muscle movement and order a specialized MRI of your eyes. Because you believe you are still in the healing process, I will have you return in six weeks and then re-measure your eye muscle movement. We shall see."

"OK," I agreed.

I saw Dr. Hoyt again in six weeks, and he was surprised to see that my eye muscle nerves were indeed still regenerating. In the end we waited until May 2, 2005 for my strabismus surgery.

A few years into our measuring and waiting together for the correct surgery timing, Dr. Hoyt had to remind me: "Be patient and wait."

I wanted to be finished with this: to stop driving to UCSF every few months, have my eye muscle surgery so I could then have my eyelid surgery, and finally be done with this seemingly endless ordeal. Inside I laughed at myself and thought: *Funny that I slowed Dr. Hoyt down in the beginning, and now in the end he's slowing me down.* Dr. Hoyt wanted at least three months of stasis—no further evidence of nerve regeneration—before he would schedule my strabismus surgery.

Sadly, Dr. Hoyt had to take a leave from work shortly before my scheduled surgery. I was disappointed for myself, and I was also concerned about Dr. Hoyt's wellbeing. I had grown to trust and to care about him. Rather than search for yet another adult strabismus specialist, I decided to have Douglas R. Fredrick,[18] Dr. Hoyt's assistant surgeon who was covering for his absence, do my surgery. It took a few appointments for Dr. Fredrick and me to communicate fully about the surgery plan: improve my upgaze as much as possible without compromising single vision in my downgaze, which I needed for reading, writing, running, and steep skiing.

I only wanted surgery on my right/injured eye. Some surgeons advised surgery also on my left/uninjured eye, to make it more synchronous with my right eye; they claimed that surgery on both eyes would increase single vision and symmetrical appearance. I learned that eyes are unique in the way they work in tandem: the optic nerve partially crosses behind the pituitary on its way to the occipital (back) lobe of the brain. I was not willing to have a completely functional eye surgically changed, because my double vision had already decreased. Also, I could see that the openness of my right eyelid as well as degree of double vision varied according to whether or not I was tired. My daughter Nicole could always see when I felt tired, because my right eyelid went to half-mast. So there could be no perfect surgical matching solution of eye functioning from what I could see—in the mirror and from inside my visual system, which varied according to sleep and stress. I knew my left eye worked 100% and I could count on it. I was now ready to see how much further improvement I could get from surgeries on my right eye, both strabismus (eye muscle) and then ptosis (eyelid) surgeries.

"You aren't black and blue at all," said Dr. Fredrick in my post-op office visit, obviously surprised by my lack of post-surgical eye bruising.

"I asked you about the safety of using a few alternative medicines just before and after the strabismus surgery. I guess they worked," I said, pleased to see from his response that my recovery from surgery was better than he had expected.

"Maybe we should do some clinical trials with this," he said.

"That's a great idea," I replied.

In the Appendix are listed all the alternative treatments and medicines I used to help facilitate my right eye opening and post-surgical healing. I hope Dr. Fredrick and other ophthalmic surgeons are doing the research that Dr. Fredrick expressed interest in: testing the impact of these adjunctive treatments in a broader sample of patients.

Six weeks after my strabismus (eye muscle) surgery by Dr. Fredrick, I had the expected ptosis (eyelid) surgery by Dr. Seiff, also at UCSF, June 15, 2005. This surgery opened my right eyelid to a more normal and symmetrical position. It was interesting to experience the surgery, because I was only partially sedated so that I could be cooperative with requests to move my eye muscles during the surgery.

I only had one surgery prior to my accident in 2000 that had required general anesthesia, and my response to the medicines after that 1999 anesthesia was horrid: severe nausea and vomiting for hours after surgery, then a bronchial spasm later in the day after I had returned home—like a severe asthma attack. I could not breathe and thought I might die because I was home alone at the moment and had no inhaler since I had never needed one. I survived that scare. Then after my emergency neurosurgery in 2000, I was closely watched because I was in the trauma ICU.

Before my first eye surgery May 2001, I had a long conversation with anesthesia department personnel, not wanting a repeat of either the nausea or the breathing problem. I was also concerned about not wanting to be medicated more than necessary, because my mother had end stage Alzheimer's after three anesthesias for three cancer surgeries in three months that had depleted her brain's "cognitive reserves" and triggered full blown dementia, from which she never recovered. I knew that my brain was vulnerable after a severe head injury, and I knew that I would probably be having three eye surgeries. I explained all these concerns to the anesthesiologist at UCSF who listened well: I woke up after the surgery feeling alert with no problems. I learned that new anesthesia drug protocols could prevent nausea, bronchial spasms, and could be done strong enough to allow surgery without pain yet light enough to wake up feeling alert. I asked for a copy of that anesthesia protocol to take with me to surgery prep appointments for my second and third eye surgeries. Those anesthesias were done in a similar way and also worked well. This kind of detailed prep and prevention before surgery was worth the effort.

I also learned in my training as a Somatic Experiencing® Practitioner that it is best for the body not to have the medication Versed in the anesthesia protocol unless really needed for some reason. (Versed was absolutely required in the clinic immediately after my accident, to get me calmed down enough to be prepared for helicopter transfer to the Reno hospital.) Versed is often given in the surgery prep area, to relax the patient and impede memory before being rolled to the surgery room. If desired by the patient, it can help not to have Versed and instead to be alert and oriented when entering the surgery room, to say "hello" to the staff there, soak in the friendly and helpful atmosphere, then close the eyelids and visualize being in a beautiful, supportive, and relaxing place while the anesthesia is given intravenously, working directly with the anesthesiologist for this timing. When I did this for later surgeries, the recovery room staff and doctors marveled at the speed and ease of my post-surgery recovery. Being alert and oriented also felt much better to me emotionally, because I was able to experience how my body felt in relation to the world around me and to understand my own sensation experiences.

After each of my second and third eye surgeries in 2005, Somatic Experiencing® hands-on expert Kathy Kain[19] gave me specific eye exercises to do post-op and then others when I got back to running. For example, while jogging on the straight section of a dirt track, I slowly rotated my right (and then left) arm from horizontal to up to horizontal position for 180 degrees, following the arm movement with my eyes as well as possible, slowing the arm movement down even more when my vision was double, as I trained my eyes to adjust and my vision to gradually become more singular. I particularly worked with my up and right lateral (to the outside) gazes, because these were the least functional. Kathy's hands-on trauma treatment and eye exercises helped me heal even further. My nerves continued to regenerate and improve for another year, more than ever expected, but not fully. Finally, in 2006 it was time for me to accept my less than perfect healing and to end my intense focus on my right eye (see Chapter 23).

My accident shifted how I see the world in two ways. I can now see well with both eyes, though not perfectly. I do have to compensate for the visual loss caused by my accident. I now have to feel where my body is in relation to everything else around me—through kinesthetic feedback—in order to navigate movement and balance through the same space I was once able to perceive visually. I still sometimes experience double vision, dependent on the position of my head, distance from my point of focus, and level of fatigue. When I do have double vision, I see the primary image more clearly than the diffuse secondary image. Having any double vision is a terrible reminder of the pains of my accident. It is a daily confirmation that no matter what I do or how hard I try, I will never be fully healed from this.

My seeing is now different on a metaphorical level as well. Nothing shakes me as deeply as before my accident. In the healing process, I have been forced to combine the nuanced feedback from my sensory organs with a fuller spectrum of emotions and intuition. I now am able to make connections that allow me to experience relationships, life, and the world in a more intense and meaningful way. I also have learned that patience is a key ingredient to healing, along with persistence, resting deeply, and holding hopeful attitude.

Zest for life is something I always associate with my dear friend Carole. On a citrus fruit the zest is the underside of the peel that has the most flavor, and when the ski accident temporarily peeled away the normalcy of Carole's life, I saw more clearly her delight in living, a delight that was present even in the catastrophe. One way I experienced Carole's zestiness was in her humor.

When I first saw Carole in her hospital room in the Bay Area, she gestured to her wet clothes hang-drying from every available door, curtain rod, and bedpost. "They're making me demonstrate my ability to do basic household chores," she said. "If I pass the test, I can go home." Noticing my quizzical look at the damp nightgowns and sweatpants, Carole bent over in laughter, revealing to me the full landscape of her wounded head. Stapled, stitched, and bruised, she was meeting life's challenges and—amazingly—finding some light in the darkness.

Weeks later I offered to drive her to a medical appointment. She was living in her home by then—apparently capable of doing laundry—and as we walked out her front door she strapped a white bicycle helmet to her fragile head. Standing on the sidewalk beside my car, she fixed me with her one open eye and sang "Happy Birthday." It was my birthday, but I had no idea she would remember it. As she added, "And many more!," I again registered Carole's zest for life. No matter what, she held on enthusiastically to what's important. Hugging her in thanks and with tears in my eyes, I told her I was moved by the sight of her all dinged up, helmeted, and belting out a song to me. Again she doubled over in laughter. The laughter returned an hour later when we noticed the startled faces of the office workers while Carole talked to them, displaying far more authority and competence than her appearance signaled.

My sense is that faith, delight, and an enduring resilience undergird Carole's humor-ready joie de vivre. As with zest, its flavor and fragrance suffuse Carole's life and many of us blessed to be near her.

Carole, remembering your capacity for humor, even as you recovered from the accident, brings sorrow and joy. I loved to see you laugh and to laugh with you. What a relief.

(Zest and Humor: Reflections for Carole, by Susan Phillips,[1] friend and colleague, 2014.)

12

Humor Helps, Too

I heard different stories about talking on the phone with friends while I was in the Reno hospital. For example:

"You were trying to tell me about something in your hospital room: *Big round things, red, yellow, and blue, hanging; but some things were soft, and also squares with writing*, as you tried to find words to tell me about what you were receiving from those of us who love you. I was confused, but I searched with you for the words you could not find, 'Big and round with colors. Do you mean balloons?' *Yeah*, you said enthusiastically, and we both burst into laughter. 'But soft?' Yeah, soft and smelly. 'Oh, do you mean flowers?' *Yeah. There are lots of 'em, and they're beautiful.* We burst into laughter again. 'Squares with writing? Do you mean post-its?' *No*. 'Hmm. Cards?' *Yeah, lots of 'em. They are so sweet and loving.*

"Then you went on to talk about different people by name, telling me stories with great specificity. What a surprise. After hearing your stories, I said, 'My brain feels a bit shocked and scrambled.' *Yeah, so does mine*, was your immediate response. *It's hard to think. It hurts.* We laughed again. I was so relieved that you could still think and talk, that we could still laugh."

I was sad to later find that none of my family or friends had taken a photo of me in the trauma ICU, when I looked really scary.

"You should have known that with my macabre sense of humor, I would want to see how I looked."

I only heard, "We did not know if you would make it. It was too horrible, and such a picture was hardly the final memory we wanted of you." Then I understood.

I heard other stories, including this one from my time at the Bay Area hospital for inpatient rehabilitation:

"You had lists. You walked fast. You were on a mission. In fact, you walked right by Lois and Bernhard, and I thought they were your parents. You were headed to a washer and dryer, doing laundry. Then you relaxed enough to talk a bit after you accomplished your tasks." We later laughed hilariously about my single-focused drive to get out of the hospital.

I looked like a punker's dream image, with shaved head, long scars, hardware (staples), dents in my head, and black eyes. I looked scary, toughened up. But I had a Disney voice—I sounded like Snow White. I wondered if I would always sound so young, how my clients would react. I could barely open my mouth, less than an inch. Trying to open it further really hurt badly.

A visit to an ENT doctor (throat specialist), after I got out of the hospital, clarified that half of one of my vocal cords was paralyzed, probably due to a rapidly done intubation boo-boo. I was told that my vocal cord might become un-paralyzed over the course of time, or maybe not. Ohhhhhhh. So I played with my weird voice and joked about it. I also consulted with a dentist who was a TMJ (temporomandibular joint) specialist and followed his advice. Weeks of three times daily hot showers, which helped the aching muscles all over my body, plus doing mouth and jaw exercises under the running hot water, finally helped my mouth to open and my vocal cord to come back to life. Whew.

Shortly after my Bay Area hospital for inpatient rehabilitation discharge, I needed to see my regular internist. My friend Susan offered to drive and accompany me. After my appointment with

Priya Yerasi,[2] who thankfully saw me clearly for my prior plus injured self, Susan asked as soon as we left the office, "Did the way people were watching you bother you?"

"I didn't even notice. I was too busy reading my hospital medical file and clarifying concerns I wanted to discuss with Dr. Yerasi." Then I laughed, "Sometimes it's better to be oblivious. What was it like? Did they look shocked?"

"Oh yes," Susan replied. "Multiple staff came to the window, and many of the patients in the waiting room watched you. I think they were all amazed that someone so wounded was functioning so competently."

"Oh my. I'm glad I didn't notice. That's why I only look in the mirror once a day: that horror is more than enough." We had a hearty laugh together at the irony.

Then I added: "When I was 14, I got such bad poison oak that my face was swollen twice its normal size, with hardened green puss. It really hurt. When my mom took me to the doctor, everyone—old and young—moved as far away from me as possible yet also stared at me. I felt like a circus freak. I was embarrassed, yet it cracked me up, even at 14. This reminds me of that weird experience." We laughed again.

Susan, one of the busiest women I know, generously volunteered to drive me to many Bay Area medical appointments. This time together deepened our friendship. Susan recently reminded me: "As we crossed Berkeley and the Bay Bridge, anyone glancing over at you in the car would have seen a bruised face, closed right eye, and old-fashioned white bicycle helmet on a passenger. They saw woundedness while I experienced you as the same, with-it, caring friend you'd always been."

"Oh yeah," I said. "Pretty weird. But, hey, my head felt fragile and I felt vulnerable, so I chose to do whatever I needed to help me tolerate returning to the free, moving, non-hospital world."

Susan is hilarious and makes me laugh. After my accident,

laughter was a much-needed antidote to my pains. I was grateful that Susan understood and shared my humor, even in tough times, so we could laugh together and laugh as often as possible.

I was told that I could not drive, that the hospital staff had reported my head injury to DMV (Department of Motor Vehicles), and my license was suspended for now. So I walked Nicole, my daughter, to school. Being 10 and fearing embarrassment, Nicole felt mortified about being seen with me by her peers. So, I wore scarves over my shaved head, and when we got within a few blocks of her school, I hugged Nicole and said, "Goodbye, Sweetheart. I love you. It was fun to walk with you. I hope you have a good day."

Then I dropped back three to five paces behind Nicole the last bit of the ¾ mile walk from home to Berkeley Arts Magnet. Meanwhile, I joked silently with myself: *You are really a 'little woman' now: you walk behind and defer to your 10 year old. Mercy.*

After following Nicole until she entered her school, I walked home without a scarf, which felt freer and less cumbersome. When I noticed funny stares, I chuckled. One time I saw a parent of a child that Nicole was close to in preschool. She acted awkward, said little, and got away from me as quickly as possible. *That was weird*, I thought to myself.

My friend Lois, who ran the preschool, later explained, "I ran into Sandy, and she asked me if you had cancer. She was shocked to see you." Then Lois and I burst into laughter at the confusion about why my head was shaved, given the scars and hardware in my head. *Oh my, it is hard to see someone bruised and battered, regardless of the cause*, I thought.

Then there was my first visit to see my acupuncturist, Lynn Segura,[3] in Berkeley. When I arrived, one of her colleagues, who I knew, stared at me with eyes wide and pupils dilated, obviously trying to figure out who I was and frightened by my appearance. When Lynn called me by my first name, her colleague gasped in horror.

When we got into a private treatment room, I joked, "What's her problem? I look far better than I did a month ago!"

"I think she was responding to all the chi (energy in Chinese medicine terms) being gone from you. The amazing thing is, you walk around with a smile on your face, apparently not at all embarrassed about your appearance. I really admire that you can do this."

"Well, I don't have to look at myself like you have to look at me." We both chuckled. "I still feel like me from the inside. And I'm happy to be alive."

Gradually, my chi was strengthened with Chinese medicine, rest, exercise, laughter, and time. It was obviously never totally sucked out of me or I would not have been able to fight for my survival, in the tree well or in the hospital.

Later when I returned to work, my eyes and brain formed a kaleidoscope of the client sitting in front of me, plastered across the entire wall behind the person. This was a most unusual visual experience and was quite disconcerting. When it first happened, after my right eyelid began to open, I silently joked with my brain: *They're after me! They're after me!* - to help me not take my problems too seriously. Then I settled down to the task at hand, my clients' feelings and concerns. Focusing now on the other, I quit noticing the kaleidoscope. Within a few weeks, my vision calmed down and was only double.

I really needed to joke and laugh after my accident, both to remember feeling good in my body and to hold a perspective beyond my personal aches and pains. Daily humor and laughter can work as therapy for coping with the effects of injury or illness, restoring a sense of well-being, as well as helping to boost the immune system.[4]

I'm so happy to be returning to my doctor, acupuncturist, and massage therapist. What a relief. They know the whole me, from long before my accident.

I'm sick of such intense physical focus on myself, including the need to meet and choose a number of new doctors. I'm overwhelmed by the number of medical problems I now have: one closed eye and then double vision, fragile balance, neck and body pain, weakness and physical exhaustion, new need for much sleep, instant menopause. It's also harder for me to spell, to remember names, and my short-term memory is not what it used to be.

I'm trying to approach my healing holistically, with Western doctors, alternative healers, and good health practices—glad I have had those all my adult life. But now I really have to work hard to get this all together, even have to work hard just to get back to my routine exercise.

Funny that I, a psychologist, who's had years of psychotherapy myself, am now focused on issues of my body, returning to work, supporting my relationships, plus reclaiming my full life. Right now, I have no time to contemplate my navel—hurt emotions, how others see me, what is related to my early life and what it all means to me now, that kind of stuff. My, how time, situations, and aging can change us. Funny how much relationships can shift after trauma, for good and for bad.

I am alive. That is very good. Where will I end up? Whole, I hope.

(Excerpt from my journal, written a month after returning home, June 2000.)

13

Healers and the Whole Person

A teenage client taught me an important word years ago, when she said, "There's only one word for a boyfriend like that: a four letter word."

"What word is that?" I asked, fully expecting a profane or harsh word, given her story.

"*Next*," was her quick response.

We both burst into laughter, and I said, "*Brilliant!*"

I learned to say "next" to doctors who boxed me in with their own expectations, and then I searched for true healers. My own healing journey provided attunement to the following characteristics that I found in *True Healers*—they know how to:

- Listen well to patients/clients and their loved ones,
- Answer questions,
- Examine thoroughly (including examination of the body by medical doctors, and not just ordering tests),
- Think creatively, and
- Hold an attitude of hope.

They also:

- Seek consultation from colleagues as needed,
- Know their personal skills and limitations,

- Help facilitate good referrals as needed, and
- Recognize and honor the skills of other true healers in providing Comprehensive Integrative Holistic Healing that is individualized for each patient/client.

In addition to my pre-accident internist, acupuncturist, and massage therapist, I eventually needed five eye doctors, a neurologist, two physical therapists, three chiropractors, a neuropsychologist/psychotherapist, professional help for my daughter Nicole and her trauma response to my accident, as well as alternative healers for my eye saga that eventually included somatic therapists.

Choosing true healers was my first step. As with any big illness or accident, choosing and then managing multiple appointments with different specialists was nearly a fulltime occupation and felt quite overwhelming. It became clear in time that it was important to be flexible and to make changes as needed along the way. My physical status changed as I began healing, so I needed different skill sets in healers. Some true healers have multiple skill sets, and no one has all skill sets.

Doctors tend to work with the issue of the day, looking at it from the viewpoint of their unique medical specialties, so taking notes and having copies of medical records helped me keep track of the whole medical picture. My internist helped me with this, too. Over the course of treatments and surgeries after my accident, I learned how important a skilled and attuned family practice physician or internist is.

Below are a few examples of the many experiences I encountered in finding true healers and then helping them work with the whole person that I am.

One of my Bay Area hospital for inpatient rehabilitation doctors wanted me to see him after discharge, though I knew I wanted to return to my trusted internist rather than be followed by the rehab staff. I also needed to return to work, and I did not want the inpatient staff to impede that as they had threatened to do if I did not cooperate with them. So I obligingly made an after discharge outpatient appointment.

He arrived late to my appointment, fumbled through papers, and said, "I can't seem to find your medical record."

"No worry," I replied. "I have copies of my hospital rehab discharge summary, as well as your dictation. Here, you can copy it. I do want to keep my copy."

He then copied and read the medical papers that I brought. He was embarrassed, awkward, and had nothing more to offer me now, though he had been helpful in the hospital.

I said, "I want to be followed by my own internist now, as well as by a neurologist—given my head injury—and a neuropsychologist who is also a psychotherapist, for evaluating me and aiding my eventual return to work."

"That sounds like a good plan," he said with a reassured tone.

"Thank you for your help in the rehab hospital unit," I said, and that was the last time I saw him.

When I saw her in May 2000, shortly after my rehab hospital discharge, my internist Priya Yerasi[1] examined my body thoroughly, talked with me about what had happened, and looked over my whole situation, including records, reports, and labs. Then she said, "I'm concerned about the functioning of your pituitary gland."

This was a concern that no other doctor had mentioned. As a nurse, I understood that the pituitary—hormone/endocrine control center i.e. "master gland"—is housed in the brain at the back of the sphenoid bone structure, the broken bones related to my right eye injury. I was thrown into instant menopause, but more about that later (in Chapter 14).

My pituitary gland was so obviously impacted that by June 2000 Dr. Yerasi said, "I'm worried that your body's immune system and capacity to respond to stress may no longer be functional. I'm going to order a cortisol test, to see if that's shut down, too. It's not a fun test, because you have to drink some nasty fluids, stay in the lab area, and have your blood drawn over time. OK?"

"Sounds wise. Thanks for being so tuned-in to what's going on with me," I replied.

Fortunately, my cortisol level was normal.

I found that it was important to get and read medical records, to help fill in the mental gaps after such a trauma experience, to aid in integrating the experience emotionally, and also to help me see the big picture of my healthcare and healing. For instance, while carefully reading my records, I learned that I bled so badly after crashing into the tree that I was given two pints of blood at Washoe Medical Center in Reno.

We all know about scary modern day blood transmitted diseases, including STDs and hepatitis. A dear friend died of AIDS in 1991 from a blood transfusion related to elective surgery in the early 1980s when HIV was just being identified. So I was very alert to this potential, and half a year after my blood transfusions, I asked Dr. Yerasi, "Wouldn't it be a good idea to do a full battery of STD and hepatitis lab work, given I have two units of foreign blood in me?"

"Yes, it would," she said. We were both relieved when my tests came back negative (normal).

Shortly after my return to Dr. Yerasi, she helped me find an intelligent, excellent neurologist: Irene Pech.[2]

After Dr. Pech's thorough examination of my neurological status and review of my records, I asked, "Wouldn't it be wise to get a baseline, post-accident brain MRI, given that only x-rays and CT scans were taken after my accident?"

"Yes, it would," she replied. We were both relieved that the results of that MRI only showed expectable changes from my accident injuries, with no sign of dementia.

Dr. Pech later carefully supervised the gradual withdrawal from my pain medication, Neurontin.[3] Subsequently, she supervised my return to exercise and helped me select alternative treatments that were safe for my spinal cord, given my pain and injuries.

My visual difficulties exacerbated my neck pain. In the tree crash, I had broken two bones in my neck (C6 and C7). Tilting my head back, to ease vision, increased neck tension and pain. I learned as a result of this pain that we have occipital muscles, strong muscles that extend from the neck up to attachments at the back of the skull. These muscles even now tend to get tight for me with any stress or certain physical movements. I have continued receiving body therapy that includes work with my occipital muscles; this enables me to ache less and stay as physically flexible and relaxed as possible.

In addition to seeing medical doctors, post-hospitalization I was doing Rehab Without Walls[4] out of my home. When the rehab staff came to my home to evaluate me, I was very pleased that they began by asking, "What rehab help do you think you need now?"

Just being asked that question felt wonderful—after my hospital for inpatient rehabilitation experience. I responded, "I think I only need physical therapy (PT) and to see a neuropsychologist to prepare me for and oversee my return to work. I insist on being able to choose the neuropsychologist, given my horrible experience with the one assigned to me at the inpatient rehab unit."

"This should be possible," the evaluators said. "But don't you also need occupational therapy (OT) and speech therapy (ST), plus a social worker (SW) to oversee your situation?"

"I don't think so," I replied.

After a full evaluation by each rehab specialist, the treatment coordinator at Rehab Without Walls agreed that I did not: "You instinctively started doing for yourself everything that OT, ST, and SW would have taught you. We will focus on PT and find a good neuropsychologist for your situation and needs."

First, a PT came to my home, and we worked together for an

hour three times a week. Soon we were rapidly navigating walks and steps at UC Berkeley (just a few blocks from my home), hopping, changing paces, testing and retraining my balance. It was challenging and difficult, yet we saw gradual improvement.

Some weeks later, we did yoga to a video in my living room. My left shoulder froze in reaction, resulting in severe pain and very limited mobility and strength.

Oh no. Give me a break. I do not need a new problem, I thought but did not say. Then I sighed, thinking: *My body is obviously more fragile and vulnerable than it was before. Horrors. When will this recovery end?*

For my new problem, I saw orthopedist Dr. George Pugh[5] who recommended and ordered a new type of PT. So I quit working with the Rehab Without Walls PT and went to an office with much equipment: Berkeley Physical Therapy,[6] where I worked with Ben Gilbert, PT, a therapist skilled in the treatment of frozen shoulders. This time I endured PT, which I dubbed "physical torture," because it felt painful. Very gradually, my shoulder range of motion and strength returned to normal functioning.

Meanwhile, I asked Dr. Pech, "Would it also be OK for me to see a chiropractor, to help with my neck and shoulder pain?" I added, "I can feel these are linked: vision difficulties affect how I position my head, which can hurt my neck. Plus my frozen shoulder might be connected to the fractured neck bones—both on my left side."

"OK, but not a chiropractor who does big manipulations. Your neck is too fragile for that," Dr. Pech replied.

So my acupuncturist helped me find a DNFT (directional nonforce technique) chiropractor, Scott Phillips,[7] who did hands-on healing, with fingers gently touching close to my spine. I was surprised to find that the pain-free, relaxing DNFT sessions did as much to release my frozen shoulder as the acupuncture and (painful) new PT did.[8] I believe this multi-modal approach was most helpful, because I got full recovery reasonably quickly even though

I had been told that many people do not completely recover after frozen shoulder.

I also asked Dr. Pech: "Is it OK if I jog again? My PT walks with Rehab Without Walls have ended, and I feel the need and desire to return to aerobic exercise."

She advised: "Return to running very slowly, on a flat dirt track, only one quarter mile for three to five days, walking before and after you jog. Pay attention to feedback from your body. Increase the distance by only 1/8 or 1/4 mile more at a time, again for three to five days in a row at the new distance, before you consider if your body feels ready to add a bit more yet again, or not."

At this painfully slow rate, it took many weeks to get back to my pre-accident hour-long jog, four to six times per week. This slow approach felt correct, and though it was hard to hold back the reins on my former marathoner self, I was grateful for Dr. Pech's wise and cautious advice that enabled me to heal my frozen shoulder and return to running without new injury.

I feel certain that this return to running furthered the full healing of my body with more oxygen available for all my cells. My rate of return to my former life sped up in a way that was unparalleled.

In addition to Western/allopathic physicians who worked with me as true advocates and healers, I also found that Eastern/alternative/complementary medicine, including body therapies and body psychotherapies, helped to rebuild my immune system and energy level as well as to release trauma reactions stored in my body.[9] This kind of Comprehensive Integrative Holistic Healing utilized the best of Western and Eastern medicine. It felt empowering to consider the healing goals and solutions I wanted, then to find practitioners who could help me reach them. In the Bay Area of Northern California where I live, there are many skilled medical specialists as well as alternative healers. In addition, complementary medicine modalities are becoming more common around the country and even being introduced as part of medical school curricula.[10]

I believe that we each have a unique Whole Person, relevant to our particular mind, body, emotions, psyche, spirit, and life experiences. I related most to loved ones who could see past my injuries during my post-accident recovery process, and to healers who could do the same or who would at least accept what I was willing to do or not do, after their disclosures about benefits, limitations, and risks of different options. My healing process was individualized, based on how my whole system was responding. This caused me to dynamically experience the interconnectedness and interplay of each aspect of my whole self. In a new way, I also experienced my interconnectedness with all others and most particularly with my loved ones, healers, and clients.

I am disgusted by the stupid questions that some people are asking me, like:

"What have you learned from this experience?"

"What have you gained from this experience?"

"Don't you think going through all this will really help you in your work and life?"

Like I really want to sit around and philosophically contemplate the "benefits" of such a terrible experience.

I wish this had never happened at all. I'm doing my best to cope and heal.

Probably the greatest benefit now is that when I feel and say "No," I really mean it and stick to it in a new way.

(Excerpt from my journal, late May after my April accident, 2000.)

14

Unexpected Benefits

It took me a long time to appreciate the real unexpected benefits from my big ski accident. I was too busy trying to heal and get back to my normal life to even imagine being able to contemplate my experience philosophically. But in time, I could not help but notice some real and surprising benefits.

Along with meeting new physicians and other healers, I learned about a broader variety of complementary healing approaches. Integrative/Comprehensive/Holistic Medicine was already an interest of mine, and this was furthered by my experience as a patient.

For example, after discharge from the Bay Area hospital for inpatient rehabilitation, I was treated by my acupuncturist Lynn Segura,[1] twice a week for two hours a session, to reclaim my energy and to strengthen my immune system's healing response. Also, hitting that tree had shattered bones in my head that affected my pituitary gland, the master gland behind the eyes that sends signals to other glands and organs such as the thyroid gland, adrenal glands, ovaries in women, and testes in men. Bonking my bones and pituitary had thrown me into instant menopause with the usual symptoms of hot flashes, difficulty sleeping, and dry mucosa. My blood hormone levels immediately changed from normal to post-menopausal. What a shock.

My first, trauma-induced menopause was relatively short-lived.

Within six months, (during which my complementary treatments included acupuncture, ancient Chinese herbs, CranioSacral therapy, and massage therapy) my hormone levels gradually returned to a normal premenopausal level, and my menstrual cycle resumed, without taking supplemental hormones.

Several years later, I went through a second round of menopause, this one slow and normal. Because I had already worked with Lynn's acupuncture and herbs on menopausal symptoms after my accident, it was simple to return to this regime, since I knew it was effective for me. This time, I did not return to pre-menopausal hormone levels as I had at 48. However, I skated through menopause with only a few hot waves (no true, dripping-with-sweat hot flashes), relatively good sleep patterns (sometimes also aided by melatonin and jin shin jyutsu[2]), and negligible mood changes while my sex hormone levels naturally waned with age.

In this twice taken, pituitary menopausal experience, I benefitted by working with both an excellent Western medical doctor (my internist) and a skilled Eastern/Chinese medicine doctor (my acupuncturist) on the same symptoms and concerns. In fact, both of these doctors suggested I take the same vitamin regime to facilitate my brain's recovery. I felt better when taking these vitamins along with the herbs from my acupuncturist: once I forgot them when I was out of town for two weeks, and I experienced more symptoms of menopause and of brain fatigue until I got home and back on my vitamins and herbs. I was able to recover from the traumatic impact of my accident and then to move easily through an age-related, normal developmental physical life change.

One time during the late summer after my accident when I had a follow-up CranioSacral Therapy (CST) appointment with Cathy Adachi,[3] (CST described in Chapter 11), she asked, "How are you?"

"Not good," I responded. "My health insurance is trying to weasel out of more than $20,000 worth of bills from my accident.

Medical companies are impatient with lack of insurance payments and are now threatening to attach my house for money. Also, I called DMV to ask about the process of returning to driving, and it turns out they did not know I had a head injury; the reporting by the hospital obviously had not happened. Now, because I asked, at the same time I'm ready to return to driving, DMV is insisting on medical records, doctor reports and verification of my readiness, plus current vision, written, and driving exams. I can't cope with all of this."

Cathy, who was doing CST bodywork to help my right eyelid open, responded, "I'm so sorry. It must feel like too much," as she gently worked with my head bones.

Suddenly, I had a flashback to the tree well: with my eyes closed I was seeing how I fought wildly and fiercely for my life. This was my first memory of the accident itself. I felt Cathy's touch and supportive presence as I went through this experience in my mind.

I had been quite anxious, on edge since my big accident. It was as if my body had remained stuck in the adrenalized poise of fight or flight. This kind of chronic anxiety was a new experience for me. I had only had two short-lived strong anxiety experiences before in my life: one related to a divorce (not chosen by me) and one to a PhD dissertation deadline when a huge snowstorm prevented access to my writing-in-progress for a crucial week.

Now I had been stuck in a physiologically anxious state since April 16, 2000, for over four months. After my CST flashback visit to the fateful tree well, I quit feeling this *constant* low-grade anxiety. I also got over my immediate acute distress about money and driving. I had seen how I fought to live, how I was helped by kind people, and then I was able to relax into my current challenges. Within a day, I laughed inside, thinking: *Freud was actually correct about some things. Now I have internally experienced something I was taught in graduate school but had a hard time believing back then. Getting more conscious awareness has quickly decreased my anxiety. Wow. I can see that I needed to have that awareness visually while experiencing it in my body with the support of a skilled hands-on practitioner. After re-experiencing my fight for life, I feel able to deal with my health insurance, my bills, and DMV, one step at a time.* This was an unexpected benefit of CST, which I sought to open my right eye.

I was happy to return to my pre-accident, relatively non-anxious coping capacity. My family was relieved, too, because they—and especially my daughter—were not used to being around me as an anxious person.

I have already described (in Chapter 11) my eye-healing saga. It felt empowering to heal my eye from the inside, with clearly visible and measureable signs of improvement in my right eye, healing the palsy of my crushed cranial nerves III and VII. It also felt wonderful to receive help from highly skilled alternative healers as well as medical doctors.

In time, I found it helpful to notice these benefits and good outcomes, to counteract the experience of a big trauma with many attendant mini-traumas. Noticing also made me more aware of both positive and challenging (so-called "negative") emotions. The most profound unexpected benefit has been the broadening and deepening of my inner landscape, giving me greater compassion for myself and for others, a sense of more meaning and purpose in my life, and a greater capacity to say and mean "no."

Alrighty then. It's becoming clear that if I want to return to my full life, I have to return to work, and sooner than later. But I'm beyond exhausted. No one is coming forward with the kind of financial help I would need, after making promises to take care of me. Guess it's a wish and not a reality; I realize this as I rest in bed much of the day and observe choices being made around me as opposed to feelings expressed to me. Hmmm.

On the other hand, I could act like a brain injured geek, give up trying to heal fully, close my practice, sell my cabin, cut out most travel and unneeded expenses, and live simply—as a disabled person. I do have disability insurance and social security insurance. And I know how to be frugal.

Hanging out sounds nice. Playing the piano sounds nice. Not pushing myself sounds nice. Not focusing on healing sounds nice.

But I'm pretty young to dial back my life in such a huge way, unless it's totally necessary. It would really be hard on Nicole. She's so young and full of life. I actually still feel a lot of life inside me. And there's so much I love about the life we've formed. It's not in my character to give up easily, especially when I don't think it's necessary.

Inner discernment. Choices. What to do? What can I do? Hmmm…

(Excerpt from my journal, mid June after my April accident, 2000.)

15

Return to Work: Challenges and Gifts

A part of me wanted not to have to return to work for months, to just focus on my healing. But I needed income, and thankfully I love my work.

Jerry, one of several friends who came to Reno soon after my accident, tried to contact some wealthy friends of mine, including through the company I had gone heli-skiing with every year for 15 years.[1] He called, told them about my accident, survival, and then asked, "Would you please give me the addresses and phone numbers of the group that Carole skis with in the Monashees? I'm sure they would want to know what's happened to her, and I'm concerned about her financial survival and seeking donations to help her out."

The company responded very professionally: "We're so sorry for Carole, and we will send her a donation to show our support for her. We cannot release contact information because it's confidential."

Jerry then suggested to other friends: "Carole could sell her house to help her survive financially."

One Berkeley friend responded: "Carole wouldn't want to sell her house unless she really needed to, and I think she'll recover and be able to work again. She also wouldn't be happy with your attempts to get her wealthy friends to donate money." This friend knew me well.

My extended family had no wealth or money to offer me. I was a single parent of a daughter, plus I own a house with a mortgage and a cabin with maintenance expenses. There was no one who could pay for all this, as well as my private practice overhead, while I focused on healing.

In that first month back home, while I always had some family or friend staying with us to help Nicole and me, which I very much appreciated, I secretly longed for someone to offer, unasked, to pay my bills for as long as I needed to focus on healing. It became clear within a month that this was not going to happen. If I wanted to keep my house, my cabin, and my lifestyle, I had to go back to work as soon as possible, to earn money for all of this. Moreover, I wanted to reclaim my full life, which includes my work. I had clients who had become emotionally attached to me during their deep psychotherapy work, and they were reeling from the news of my accident. Some were being seen by colleagues until I could return to work.

Since I work for myself, I had no sick leave, except for my savings. I did have private disability insurance, which only kicks in 90 days after a clear disability; and I had social security insurance, which would kick in if I were deemed totally disabled. From these I could have opted to receive nearly $4,000 a month, tax free, until age 65; then the social security portion would continue for the rest of my life. I had been injured very badly, and I knew I could cover up my inner health and get this money, if I wanted to. Besides, the hospital inpatient rehab doctors had presumed this was my story, period, the end.

I did not want to live the injured, disabled life or believe I had to do so. After calculating simplified expenses, I knew that I could milk the system and never work again. I even let myself imagine how I could play out the "too mentally injured and sick to work" role. But I loved my life and my work too much to do that. So I chose to return to work as I had chosen to seek full healing—because I wanted to and intuitively believed that I could.

I knew I needed to be supervised by a neuropsychologist clinician while returning to my private practice as a clinical psychologist. The Bay Area hospital for inpatient rehabilitation doctors had threatened my professional license, saying: "We believe you might never be able to return to your work, to be a psychotherapist again. Your brain injury was too severe and extensive. You have frontal and prefrontal lobe damage, cannot judge your limitations or handle complex problem solving. And if we learn that you return to work soon against our assessment and suggestion, you will be reported to the Board of Psychology."

I did not agree with the hospital rehab facility neuropsychologist's assessment of my mental status. But aside from these threats, I knew that in order to ethically protect my clients as well as myself during the process of returning to work, I needed outside feedback to make certain I was thinking clearly.

I had skillfully disconnected from the Bay Area inpatient rehabilitation staff after my hospital discharge, then continued with Rehab Without Walls in Berkeley, where I met and chose to work with Carrie Thaler, a neuropsychologist who was also a psychotherapist.[2] I was grateful that my health insurance agreed to pay for this, as part of my occupational rehab, because all the complementary/alternative treatments I was seeking—most of which are not covered by my health insurance—were increasing my medical expenses tremendously.

I started seeing clients very slowly, under the supervision of Dr. Thaler. I saw her twice a week as I initially returned to work. I was relieved that when I discussed my work, Dr. Thaler gave me excellent feedback, such as, "These are very complex clinical situations. You are handling these as well as any psychologist could."

I saw Dr. Thaler for seven months, until she and I were both satisfied that her supervision of my return to work was no longer necessary. I also discussed cases and got feedback from friends who are clinical psychologists, even after seeing Dr. Thaler.

I had some tough clinical situations. For example, one was a woman who had shown up at the rehab unit, uninvited and unannounced, catching me by surprise in the hallway near my hospital room. She later explained: "I needed to make certain you really had had an accident and were not just trying to get rid of me." Another was a couple about whom I was deeply concerned, whose marriage was falling apart in a complicated way at the time of my accident.

There were some individuals and couples who were in therapy with colleagues during my hospitalization and rehabilitation, needing help sooner than I could provide. They needed to be transitioned back to me in clinically astute ways, to help heal the trauma my accident had triggered in them. Some of this process was made more difficult by misconceptions of me that the inpatient neuropsychologist communicated to some of my colleagues. If the frontal, prefrontal, and parietal lobes of my brain were really not working properly, then I should not return to my professional work. But I was able to sort this out with colleagues and transition back to work with all my clients except one couple. I understood the complicated reasons for no longer doing psychotherapy with that couple. Though I disagreed with that plan, understanding the dynamics enabled me to let go without confrontation—yet one member of the couple was not happy about it, so I had a helpful closure session with that person after I returned to work.

In addition to my usual challenging work as a clinical psychologist, I needed to help my clients cope with the trauma my accident had created for their psychotherapy, in order to return to the concerns that had caused them to seek therapy: to focus on their own healing processes. Moreover, I needed to cope with colleagues' misconceptions of me, as well as my own brain echoes of the hospital inpatient rehab doctors' view of my incapacity to work. Dr. Thaler helped me with all of this, as I reclaimed my clinical competence. Close colleagues helped me, too.

One consequence of my accident and return to work was my decreased energy. I had a number of clients with whom I deeply resonated and who kept their need of me to our scheduled sessions, except in very unusual and infrequent crises. I had a few clients about whom I also cared very deeply, yet they took more mental and emotional energy as well as time than all the others combined due to their early developmental traumas and needs; I was now too exhausted to treat these people effectively. Dr. Thaler helped me see and accept this. Then I consulted with a psychologist attorney[3] about the legally and therapeutically correct way to transition these clients to another psychotherapist given my accident and their needs, and Dr. Thaler helped me with the clinical details of the discussion and referral process for each client.

After transitioning these few people to other professionals, I told Dr. Thaler: "This was hard for me to do. I didn't want to let these people down, because I care about them. But I really needed to do this for my own health *and* for theirs, given my accident and current energy level. Frankly, it's a tremendous relief to let go and provide good referrals, to accept and own my limits, to de-stress my work life. Thank you for helping me see and do this."

I worked more than full time before my accident, but I was happy to work less than full time after my accident. It was all I could manage. My own healing took many hours of treatments with both doctors and alternative healers every week. I was also helping my daughter recover from the trauma my accident caused her, plus coping with and rebuilding the rest of my life.

In order to allow adequate time for comprehensive healing, I let go of all areas of my work as a psychologist beyond a modified, part-time private practice. I quit supervising psychotherapists in their pre-licensure training process. I quit teaching graduate school courses, offering workshops, and leading retreats. I felt both sad and relieved in response to decreasing and simplifying my work demands.

One interesting effect of returning to work was the probable benefit for my brain functioning. I had to use my mind in order to once again perform my professional tasks. I was concerned about my clients, love my work, and wanted to reclaim this aspect of my life. Also, I needed money. So I returned to work within a few months, albeit at a moderated pace. Six years later I had to undergo extensive neuropsychological testing for a lawsuit that I had initiated (but that is another story, in Chapter 21). This neuropsych testing was painful to go through. I had studied neuropsych assessment for three years in graduate school, and while being tested this time, I experienced from inside out that my brain was still not functioning as it had before I hit that tree. For instance, I had been very superior at visual spatial reasoning and now I was only average. Yet I was pleased to learn that those functions most needed for my work, such as complex problem solving and other executive brain functions including reasoning and decision-making, were functioning in at least the superior range. Was this just good luck, the result of collateral circulation built from years of aerobic exercise, an example of the amazing plasticity of the brain, or a combination of all these factors? It also is entirely possible, given what we currently know about nerve regeneration and brain retraining, that my early return to work and to other cherished and demanding activities may have helped my brain adapt and relearn to function, despite the injuries caused by slamming into that tree.[4] And my accident helped me simplify and de-stress my work life.

Like Carole, my entry into the world of trauma began with a catastrophic event; for me it was a roll over car accident in which I nearly lost my left hand, leading to 16 surgeries over five years. It was soon after one of the early procedures, with my arm braced and heavily bandaged that I attended a professional workshop at Esalen[1] *led by Peter Levine. Little did I know that experience would change the course of my life. Dr. Levine took one look at me and, though I appeared to be coping well after my injury, he recognized my body physiology remained in a state of shock. During that one session he gently took me back through the accident sequence, where his remarkable attention to my sensations and images brought to light my body's attempts at self-protection that had been interrupted and rendered incomplete. As I became more consciously aware at the level of my physiology I also realized I was confronting my own near-death experience, which had never completely dawned on me before. Toward the end of that session my body proceeded to enter into a deep state of rhythmic shaking, which signaled the shock energy had been re-activated and was beginning to make healthy release. Overall I was stunned to discover all that had been going on in my body outside my usual awareness. As I rested afterwards, these newly found feelings of deep safety and settling comforted me and showed where my further recovery would take me.*

I undertook my training in Somatic Experiencing®, partly to offer my own clients these methods to renegotiate their trauma, and partly to deal with the impending surgeries to reconstruct my hand. I saw profound results as their fight/flight energy was unbound from the nervous system, allowing the individual to make remarkable recovery from stubborn behavioral and emotional symptoms previously resistant to even excellent psychotherapy. Their resulting vitality and resilience showed the efficacy of a mind-body approach. Incidentally I had ample opportunity to use these methods myself with each new surgery, and my wonderful surgeon became a fan as he saw the speed of my recovery and reduction of customary pain.

Carole's journey, and my own, reflect how this powerful process of working with the body's natural self-regulating systems can in fact become transformative, not only promoting healing from discrete trauma, but also deeper changes in underlying patterns of nervous system dysregulation—including my own tendency to operate at maximum capacity with little room for rest. Obviously, being mindful and making necessary changes in life balance reduce chances of new trauma. Despite the challenges presented by my own injury and its consequences, I find myself deeply grateful for the personal and professional change that has come about from my contact with the SE™ approach and the greater level of peace and ease it has brought into my life.

It has been especially meaningful to share SE™ with Carole. Prior to her accident I had been able to help many clients with this method. But this was the first time that a close friend had experienced major trauma and I sensed Carole would make great use of SE™. Indeed she did. It's been like being a medical researcher studying a certain problem, then discovering a close friend who can benefit from that treatment so that part of her healing is to study the method herself and eventually join the research team. I love sharing this bond with Carole and how this has given me greater insight into her recovery.

(Reflection by Marcia Black,[2] friend and colleague, 2014.)

16

Healing From Inside Out

I feel like a total beginner. I'm a seasoned psychologist, and it seems that's at least part of the problem in learning SE™. It's a very different way of being with people and doing therapy.

Then there's my head injury, the impact of that on learning something new. At least I understand the physiology being taught, because of my nurse training. I'm used to tuning into my body, because I'm an athlete. But this is a distinct kind of tuning in: it's so much more nuanced.

Stick with this, Carole. It's good to exercise your mind as well as your body. This could be a natural way for you to practice more of your belief in holistic healing. And it's interesting and fun, even if challenging and difficult.

Timing is perfect, too. Nicole is in high school, and you're both studying a lot. You will soon be having eye surgeries, so receiving somatic help for surgery prep and recovery will be a natural for the requirement of receiving sessions. It's also likely the upcoming surgeries and SE™ sessions will trigger trauma still left in your body from the ski accident, not to mention other things in your life. Good to have the opportunity to work this through more deeply.

Scary and exciting to be embarking on this whole new approach.

(Pep talk written to myself, excerpt from my journal, spring 2005, after my April 2000 accident.)

Five years after my big accident, I began training in a type of therapy that helped integrate what I had learned as a nurse and psychologist, along with 53 years of living—full of small and large traumas. It challenged my brain to learn new and different ways of helping people, even though I had been a helping professional for over 30 years.

Somatic Experiencing® (SE™) is a body healing approach developed by Peter Levine.[3] The SE™ approach provides unique ways of helping people process trauma through their bodies, by attunement and tracking of sensations via talking as well as through body movement and touch. Dr. Levine's theory, which he developed from observations of animals in the wild, postulates that trauma causes dysregulation of the autonomic ("automatic") nervous system (ANS); and sometimes the ANS needs help to be restored, allowing the body's innate capacity for healing and self-regulation. I studied SE™ for four years, and I continue to receive consultations and take advanced workshops.

Learning SE™ has been a gift as well as a challenge. Being an athlete and a nurse, I have always been interested in the mind-body connection. Being a psychologist, I am interested in helping others and myself get through traumatic experiences. Adding SE™ to my repertoire of treatments has also helped with my own inner attunement, though I was already an intuitive person with strong awareness of feelings, reinforced by my training as a psychologist. SE™ training enhanced my ability to notice and respond to detailed sensations and feedback throughout my body.

With greater self-attunement, I now do my best to get enough sleep. I take more time to relax and to be quiet. I prefer more extended time when relating to others along with open times of not being bound to an endless schedule of promised activities. I no longer take satisfaction in being able to put huge effort into plowing through things, which I needed to do in order to support myself financially while getting my PhD. I realize now that in many ways my over-work habit was still stuck On, long after I had finished graduate school. I had become skilled at taking time for family and friends, fun, play, sports, cultural entertainment, cooking, travel, and spiritual learning. But I had not adequately learned the ways my body needed to rest and relax.

After my big accident I *had* to slow down. I learned that moving more slowly, without multi-tasking, is a more comforting way for me to experience my own aliveness. It allows me to experience fully what is going on in the moment and in the world around me. It also helps me be more accessible to and easy with others.

In addition, thanks to my own increased SE™ attunement, I feel more quickly when an interaction with another is not good for me. I use this "felt sense" information to assess the situation and take space as needed. Then I am able to choose more clearly how I want to respond, so that I can focus on facilitating the best interaction and outcome possible, given who I am and who the other person is. In this way, my body really talks to me and gives me a whole new way of understanding myself.

Studying SE™ also increased my capacity to help others as well as myself by:

- Tuning inside and noticing body sensations with connected images, emotions, behaviors, and meanings;
- Slowly processing all of this in a "titrated" (measured) way that allows
- Releasing of trauma stored in the body and brain, both with physical movements and verbal expressions.
- Then "renegotiating" stuck and imbedded experiences and memories from a sense of internal safety that enables
- The capacity to respond to one's current needs and limits providing

- A new and positive experience that feels coherent, congruent, and empowered from deep inside the whole self, including mind, emotions, body, behavior, and spirit.

I have described some of my experiences receiving SE™ as a client in Chapters 11 and 22. There are more details about how I got acquainted with SE™ in Chapters 17 and 22. There are excellent detailed books and articles on healing via SE™ (see Notes and Resources).[4] For all of this, I am grateful.

At 10 years of age, they told me I was too young to watch my mother die. My mom's accident comes back to me now in pieces, chunks of time I am unable to string together ... She's skiing down the course. 'Hurry, mom! Hurry!' She falls. She doesn't get up. 'Mom! Hurry up! We're going to lose!' No movement. Panic. I'm running up the hill to see what's going on. Two people collide with me, knock the wind out of me. They hold me back while I struggle. Are they my coaches? "Get off! Get off of me! No! No!" Ski patrol. She's gone. Into the ski clinic. Tubes, tanks, ski suit cut open, eye shut. Ghost? Zombie. Helicopter in the sky. 'She's dead. I know she's dead.' Car ride to Reno. Silence. My friend gives me the bead we had been fighting over while making jewelry last night. Confirmation that she's dead. Reno. Jerry. Craig. 'Why the hell are they here?!' Uncles. People. So many people. Easter. No candy or bunny stuffed animals for me. I clean while the little kids eat chocolate. Making a bracelet at someone else's house while I sit on a swing. Alone. ... Berkeley. No Mom. Seeing mom in rehab. 'She's going to make it.' Compassion from family friends—the first I've felt in weeks. My faux grandmother[1] and I walk down the street—the first time I've felt like I'm home.

My mom's accident haunted me every day for years, and, even after I thought I had dealt with it, it would sometimes creep up, unaware, and slam me right back down onto that ski hill. The year after the accident is a bit of a blur, much like the accident itself. What I do remember is that I was angry. Angry with my coaches who held me back from her on the hill, angry with Jerry for coming back into our lives like he had never left, angry with Craig—like he knew my mom and me better than I did. But mostly, I was angry with my mom. I didn't understand how she could do this to me. I didn't understand how she could put me through all of this. For a month, I felt completely alone. Even after my mom got out of the rehab unit, I felt like she could leave me again at any moment. I know these feelings of anger toward my mom weren't rational. She would never have chosen this for herself, or for me. But, in my traumatized state, she had been dead, she had left me, so she was the one to blame.

Once back in Berkeley, I had a good support network of family friends who did everything they could to help me. I don't know what I would have done without them, and I don't know what I would have done without my faux grandmother (who ran my preschool and is a dear friend). She was loving, caring, and brutally honest. I felt like she was the only person not tip-toeing around me, around my feelings—exactly what I needed. She would let me rage, let me yell, let me vent, she would console me, and then she would plop me back into reality. To this day, she hasn't changed.

After a lot of therapy, after my mom started getting back to her normal self, and after feeling like there was some stabilization in my life, my constant fear that my mom would leave me again began to ebb. Now I feel like I have dealt with her accident and am continually moving forward. That being said, my mom's few limitations—chiefly memory lapses—are still the main source of our disagreements. These are reminders that, no matter how much I want it to, her accident will never completely be a thing of the past. I am so thankful for the love and care shown to me by our friends, and also by my mom. If it were not for her understanding, I honestly have no idea where I would be right now.

Memories of her accident do still crop up every once in a while, but they are just that: memories. They don't affect me as much as they once did. They are now a reminder of how precious life is and how important it is to love, wholeheartedly love, while we are still here.

(Recollection of accident written by my daughter, Nicole Petiet,[2] 2014.)

17

Trauma from Trauma: Helping My Daughter

I fought so hard to live in that tree well on April 16, 2000, because of my love for Nicole. She was only ten years old then, still really needing her mom. Nicole's father had been estranged from her since she was eight. I was a single mom and strongly motivated to complete my parenting of Nicole.

It quickly became clear that my accident had traumatized Nicole. This often happens to children who experience loss. In my work as a psychologist, I sadly have seen that adults are often so caught up in their own losses that they forget to attune to the unique experiences and needs of children. Often children are left to fend for themselves emotionally in the aftermath of illness, accident or death of a family member.

I live in a complex network of friendships and extended family. Both friends and family came forward immediately to be with Nicole and to help her, not knowing if I would survive when I was in critical condition, or if I would ever be able to parent Nicole again even if I lived (given my head injury). All the adults around me—friends and family—were traumatized by my visage. One moment I had been a vibrant, healthy, active woman and the next I was close to being snuffed out, physically and mentally. I required trauma stabilization, neurosurgery, and machines to keep me alive. So it is easy to understand that nothing short of having her mom as before would have felt like enough for Nicole, especially since it was spring break and Easter, a usual time of fun and vacation for us. Instead of playing in Paris together as planned, Nicole was staying with friends in Carson City, Nevada, so she could visit me daily in the Reno Hospital the first week. Nicole then stayed with friends and family in Berkeley while she returned to school (4th grade) after spring break, until I got out of the Bay Area hospital for inpatient rehabilitation on May 12, 2000, nearly four weeks later.

As traumatized kids are, Nicole was fearful, sad, angry, and doing her best. I have heard from adult friends that Nicole was afraid of being close to me physically in the trauma unit, when I was bandaged head to toe and attached to machines. I have heard from Nicole that in the trauma unit the adults would not let her touch me, fearful for my safety.

Years after my accident, Nicole said: "Mom, I just wanted to be close to you. I needed my mommy. But I was not allowed to touch or hug you. And I hated them for this."

I have no memory of this time in Reno. I only know that the two stories are emotionally disparate: a not uncommon experience for children, especially those affected by trauma. Their felt sense often does not match those of adults around them. And they also pick up the anxiety of others.

When Nicole visited me at the Bay Area hospital for inpatient rehabilitation, fear, sadness, and a desire to please me were visible in her whole appearance and behavior. I opened my eye, while still in the cage of the fully enclosed Vail bed, and heard Nicole say, "Mom, look at the great sushi and organic salad we made for you," as she held the food out toward me yet held herself back from me.

I reached out and beckoned Nicole, "It's so wonderful to see you. I miss you. And this delicious food is helping me survive being in the hospital. I can't thank you enough. It means the world to me. You know how much I love sushi and salad."

"I brought some of your favorite chocolate, too."

"Hooray! You know what a chocoholic I am. Please come closer so I can at least hold your hand from this zoo cage bed." As I joked and tuned into Nicole, she visibly relaxed.

Soon I was out of the cage and we could hug. These visits helped fuel my desire and courage to do all I could to return home and resume our life together.

After my discharge from the hospital for inpatient rehabilitation, Nicole was afraid to be seen with me in public, particularly around her peers. Kids can be cruel and taunting when uneasy, and my very odd appearance even made adults feel uncertain about how to act or what to say. Some stared with mouths agape. Later, some adults shared their previously unspoken thoughts with me, after I looked more normal: "Does she have cancer?" (shaved head), "Is she close to dying?", "Should I ask or would that be rude?", "Should I offer help?" If adults responded with fear and mute discomfort, of course Nicole and other kids were fearful of me and responded in kid-like ways.

This is an example of mirror neurons,[3] seen on modern brain imaging with MRI and PET/CT scans, described in the research of Daniel Siegel, Bessel van der Kolk, Allan Schore, and others. Kids' minds, bodies, and emotions pick up on the emotions of adults around them. Kids do best around calm, gentle emotions with clearly held boundaries regarding behavior. When around anxious adults, kids feel anxiety. And kids are more likely to act out any felt inner trauma rather than to speak it, because kids live in the now, and that is what is going on now. So I wonder how much my anxious state affected Nicole the first weeks and months after my accident.

I was not surprised that Nicole was fearful and sad. I did my best to listen to her and support her. But I was surprised by her anger with me. I have memories of her hitting me and screaming in anger. This hurt my body, which still felt vulnerable and fragile, so I took hold of her hands, looked into her eyes, and said, "Talk to me. It's not OK to hit me. Talk to me, including about your anger." She had a short fuse, burned out by the horrific events, fear of losing me, worrying about where and with whom she would live, terrified that I might never return to the mom she had known.

I later realized it was natural for a ten year old to be angry about having to endure all of this, without any feeling of control over the cause or the outcome. With my current understanding through SE™, I can see that her anger was a good sign, an attempt to fight the trauma she experienced in herself and in me, in an instinctual way, reflexively trying to overpower it and get her life back to normal with me. I did not understand that when it happened, five years before I began studying SE™.[4]

At the time, I was happy to be alive and reclaiming my life, despite others' predictions. I had my own angers with some of the staff at the hospital for inpatient rehabilitation and with some aspects of the U.S. healthcare system, plus a few individuals who did hurtful things before and after my accident. I thought I had arranged, even while I was still in the hospital, for Nicole to be well cared-for. But the trauma response is not rational; it is a fight-flight-freeze instinctive response aimed at survival. Nicole was in fight mode. She was angry.

Close adult friends reached out to Nicole, to give her time for individual conversation and fun, to give me time to rest. For instance, eight days after my discharge from the inpatient rehab unit, our friend Mima[5] took Nicole to her art studio for some fun, creative time together. Nicole seemed happier when Mima brought her home.

Two days later, as I was walking Nicole to school, she said: "Mom, the night before I went to Mima's, I had a terrible dream: *You went blind in your open eye. Then you went completely deaf. Then you lost your voice. Then you died a week later. I had to go live in Canada with my dad; it was awful. I hurt so bad that I died in my sleep. Then my dad died the next day.* I told Mima about this dream when we were doing art, and then we had a really good talk."

"I'm so glad Mima was there for you and that you had this time with her. What a total nightmare."

"Mom, when I said goodbye at the ski clinic, I thought it was *goodbye forever*," sputtered Nicole between sobs.

I held Nicole in my arms. "Poor darling. No wonder you've been so agitated. I'm so glad that I'm still here for you. I love you. I really love you."

In two weeks, as soon as I could get an appointment for Nicole, I took her to see a pediatrician, Joan Lovett,[6] who was skilled in behavioral medicine and did some multifaceted EMDR (Eye Movement Desensitization and Reprocessing)[7] work with Nicole. This aimed to help Nicole integrate her trauma caused by my trauma. EMDR was developed by Francine Shapiro and initially was used to help Vietnam War veterans. Much research has found that EMDR is an efficacious treatment for post-traumatic stress. I had studied EMDR with Francine Shapiro before Nicole was born. Nicole, being a normal child, was more interested in friends than EMDR, so her treatment was relatively brief. Dr. Lovett's sessions with Nicole included my presence and participation in the room, were multifaceted and poignant, and Nicole seemed less acutely distressed and angry after six sessions.

Despite her anger, Nicole had also been generous and giving with me. In addition to providing healthy foods for me, Nicole made some beautiful cards and expressed her love to me.

The evolution of Nicole's trauma from the time of my accident through high school—over eight years—shows common threads of how childhood trauma manifests during crucial developmental stages.

A little over a year after my accident, Nicole experienced

images of scary people—she was convinced of ghosts—in our home. She was unwilling to move about the house without literally being attached to me and to my clothes, for weeks. No amount of reassurance or reason helped Nicole. It took much time and energy from me, and I was exhausted from work, medical/healing appointments, and endless household and parenting chores. I was also worried about Nicole's mental state. I had never experienced anything like this.

As an illustration of how childhood trauma reactions can be traumatic for others who are around the child, including adults, I share one of my failures: one day in exasperation, frustration, and with a bit of devilish play (learned by growing up with three brothers), plus a desire to scare the fear out of her and to show her there was no one there except me at the time, I surprised Nicole by jumping out and saying "Boo." Nicole screamed and cried. I felt horrible, apologized, held her, and tried to reassure her. I realized that my behavior was a stupid and bad thing to do and regretted what I had done. Nicole was already exhibiting signs of inner terror, and she did not need to have her mom scare her.

Fortunately, shortly after my unskillful reaction to Nicole's hanging onto me, I was talking with my friend Marcia Black[8] who had already begun studying SE™. She said, "Carole, why don't you get her some SE™ focused trauma treatment? I think this is a child's response to trauma."

"What? How?"

"Think about it. She's terrified about letting go of you. She won't let you out of her sight. She's afraid some horrible, unknown figure is going to harm her. Isn't that a childlike mirror of what she must have experienced when you had your accident? She's not sure she is safe, or you are safe, so she is holding on with all her might, out of trauma and fear."

"Wow. I never would've thought of that. It has felt like a crazy manipulative ploy to control my every move. But she's still traumatized by my accident?"

"And by the fear of losing you. It makes sense. This could be a new manifestation of that fear."

Marcia made referrals, and Nicole saw Ariel Giarretto, SEP.[9] Ariel did a masterful job of working with Nicole, and the scary images became a thing of the past. This was a tremendous relief to Nicole, and to me.

Nicole's temper was shorter than before, yet she was quickly approaching adolescence (coping with hormonal surges and body changes, as well as complicated peer group interactions and pressures). Fortunately, Nicole had brilliant, emotionally tuned in teachers at Berkeley Arts Magnet through 6th grade.

Then Nicole was accepted to attend Julia Morgan School for Girls (JMSG)[10] during middle school (7th and 8th grades). JMSG's motto was "preparing the capable, creative, confidant, and compassionate women of tomorrow." Nicole still recites that motto. JMSG helps its young women navigate the tumultuous middle school years by focusing on academics and teamwork. Nicole later described that she learned a tremendous amount, even more than in high school, thanks to the great teachers and approach at JMSG (middle school is often a time when girls learn relatively little).[11] [12]

At 13, Nicole joined Patch Adams,[13] her favorite instructor at Camp Winnarainbow,[14] on a trip to Russia where they did clowning for sick, dying, and orphaned children. This was a powerful, positive emotional experience for Nicole, filled with giving and receiving love.

Nicole then went to Berkeley High School (BHS), a large (slightly under 4,000 students then), diverse, inner city, coed public school. This was quite a change from her 133-student all-girls private middle school. Joining the crew team at BHS helped Nicole feel connected. It also gave her a positive athletic focus outside ski racing, which she had chosen to give up after my accident.

Interestingly, a number of the strongest girls on the BHS crew team were from JMSG.

In 10th grade, Nicole acted out with me in some unique ways. By this time, I was studying SE™ and saw her behavior as another adolescent-specific manifestation of the trauma of my accident, prompted and fueled by depositions, including hers, and the final stages of my lawsuit regarding the accident (see Chapter 21) that apparently triggered PTSD,[15] given her behavior. I got a family therapist[16] for us and another attuned and skilled SE™ therapist—Julia Gombos[17]—for Nicole. Nicole settled down within a few months, completed her high school rowing career at Oakland Strokes, finished Berkeley High a semester early, and fulfilled her dream of being recruited to a Division I collegiate rowing program. Then Nicole worked during the time that would have been her last semester of high school to save money, to help cover expenses for a summer backpack and Eurail Pass trip in Europe between high school and college.

These stories about Nicole show how severe illness, accident, or loss of a parent is traumatic to children. In Nicole's case, it required three different trauma-based treatments over the course of six years (EMDR in 2000, SE™ in 2002, family therapy and SE™ in 2006), plus some individual psychotherapy during her college years. The healing needs of children can vary as developmental stages change. Even though I—and my close friends—were attuned to Nicole's needs, she needed professional help. This is common when children experience intense trauma at such a young age.[18]

Nicole's synopsis of her experience: "It can take a long time, utilizing different types of interventions, for children to heal."

April 16, 2000, is forever etched in my memory: the day I answered the phone and heard that Carole had been in a serious ski accident and was in ICU in Reno with life threatening injuries. The odds seemed stacked against her survival, much less recovery.

For the 22 years I had known Carole, I had always experienced her as one who lives both from her head and heart, one who loved life with a joyful and contagious passion. In light of such grave injuries, I wondered if she would be able to recover and reclaim her life, if that deep love of life and her bottomless love for her daughter would give her the incentive, courage, determination and strength to work to reverse the grim prognosis.

Medical science has made huge advancement in understanding the complexities of the human body, has developed sophisticated interventions to enhance healing from injury and trauma. But how often are intangible variables such as faith, hope or love ever mentioned in a treatment plan? Yet one may choose to have faith in the efficacy of a medical procedure, hold hope for a positive outcome and be open to receiving loving support.

Carole had always been one through whom love flowed abundantly out into the world, her actions blessing many. She was the one who, when my husband was diagnosed with a rare bone marrow disorder, orchestrated an elaborate plan to gather close women friends from near and far to surprise me. I came down the stairs one morning and there to my utter amazement, they were all quietly waiting to whisk me off on a sun splashed day, for a time of laughter and deep sharing, feasting on a gourmet picnic at Love's Beach, relaxing on warm sand as we listened to each other and the quiet lapping of waves. A day never to be forgotten.

Now Carole was in a different position, vulnerable and dependent, needing to be open to receiving love as she had never experienced before. Love flowed to Carole in myriad, creative ways from family, friends, colleagues providing a lifeline as she struggled to make her way back to her full life. Would she be able to accept help given through love?

I believe that love made a huge difference in Carole's healing and recovery. As she both received and gave love, love sustained her … keeping her connected to the meaningful, supportive relationships in her life and to the mystery of the Transcendent.

(Reflection by Mima Baird,[1] friend and colleague, 2014.)

18

Lifted by Love

1 Corinthians 13

Love

1 Though I speak with the tongues of people and of angels, if I have no love, my speech is no more than a noisy gong or a clanging bell.

2 Though I have the gift of prophecy, and understand all mysteries, and all knowledge; and though I have all the faith needed to move mountains—if I have no love, I am nothing.

3 Though I may give away everything I have to feed the poor, and even give up my body to be burned—if I have no love, it does me no good.

The Qualities of Love

4 Love is patient and kind; love envies not; is not jealous, conceited, or puffed up;

5 Love is not ill-mannered, selfish, or irritable; love does not keep a record of wrongs;

6 Love is not happy with evil, but is happy with the truth;

7 Love never gives up; love believes all things, hopes all things, and endures all things.

The Permanence of Love

8 Love is eternal and never fails: but whether there be prophecies, they shall fail; whether there be tongues, they shall cease; whether there be knowledge, it shall vanish away.

9 For our gifts of knowledge and of inspired messages are only partial;

10 But when that which is perfect is come, then that which is in part will disappear.
11 When I was a child, I spoke as a child, I understood as a child, I thought as a child; but now that I am an adult, I put away childish things.
12 For now we see in a mirror dimly; but then we shall see face-to-face. What I know now is only partial; then it will be complete—as complete as God's knowledge of us.
13 Meanwhile, these three remain: faith, hope, and love; but the greatest of these is love.

(Combination of King James[2] and Good News[3] Bibles, adapted by Carole Petiet, at ages 10 and 21.)

Having grown up the daughter of missionaries in China, I was well versed in the Bible. I even combined translations so that I made up my own versions of passages that felt special, until they spoke directly to my heart. The famous passage on Love, I Corinthians 13, has been my favorite Bible chapter since I was a young girl.

I never shared that specific information about myself with Nicole.[4] I was focused on doing my best to raise her to be her best self. So I was surprised when Nicole returned home on break after her first semester in college, and I noticed something on her wrist.

"What's that?" I asked.

"I got a tattoo. You never would let me do it when I lived at home. But don't worry: it's small and not visible under my watch band, so it won't be a problem with work."

"What does it say? Why did you do it?"

"I Cor 13:8," was her reply.

"As in Corinthians, from the Bible?"

"Yeah. That's my favorite verse in the Bible, and in the King James Version. I put it there to help me remember always about the power and permanence of real love."

"Wow. Thank you for sharing this with me." Then I told Nicole about my connection with I Corinthians 13, too.

Receiving love after my accident brought joy amidst the tragedy. It was love that gave me hope, faith, and the courage to do all the hard work required to recover, to live a full life again.

Trauma provides a natural sorting of friends and family: those who respond and tune in helpfully versus those who do not. Relationships tend to deepen through shared experiences or to become less meaningful. This happens as a side effect of any big life event, including accidents, illnesses, and sometimes even surgeries. We then have the experience of learning who we can count on and what kinds of help we might need.

Family, friends, and colleagues gathered after my big accident to help protect and support me in the hospital and upon my return home. They first provided healing presence and loving touch, later added yummy and healthy food that helped rebuild my body. They helped sort out my physical and financial needs, as well as Nicole's needs. Friends provided much needed logistical and legal advice, too. Groups of people also prayed for my healing.

Some friends held the memory of medical problems that needed follow-up after the trauma unit, discussing these with me and my rehab staff. A few sent gifts of money. Many sent cards, letters, flowers, and balloons. Some protected my home and independence. Others helped me physically, including by walking with me and by finding, cleaning, mending, and building things for me. Friends helped me joke and laugh, a much needed remedy for the pain of my accident. A number stepped up to be with Nicole, for fun times as well as caretaking. Ten year old kids do need to play and have fun, especially after such a trauma in the family. Nicole got relief from the focus on day to day challenges when she was accompanied at amusement parks, water parks, playgrounds, art rooms, nature parks, concerts, plays, and movies, plus gatherings with other kids.

A number of friends drove me to appointments, all over the

greater Bay Area, as I sought advice and experts for help with continued problems after my hospitalization. I could not drive because of my head injury, so I had a crash course in mobility dependency, a hard issue eventually faced by most elderly as well as severely injured persons. I now know from experience how tough this feels. I was somewhat surprised by who stepped up to help with transportation and who did not. Friends who provided transportation made me feel that they relished sharing their time with me. This generosity amazed me and provided true lovingkindness; with ample time to talk and share, it increased the intimacy of our relationships.

Also, there was Craig, my ski friend of 13 years, who quietly held my hand as he sent love and reassurance to me in the trauma unit. He helped the inpatient rehab staff remember my bigger medical picture because he had talked with my Reno surgeon and doctors. He actually saw me as the beautiful and whole woman he had known before my accident. He reflected back my full, intelligent, strong, vital self. He helped me to feel loved and beautiful from the inside out, despite my appearance. It felt easier to resonate in his positive reflection than to actually cope with my reflection in the mirror. With Craig's positive resonance to the full me before I crashed into that tree, I actually felt like myself, albeit with a more aching body and needing to take more time to do everything. While some others tried to diminish me, Craig's loving reflection of me and loving touch helped me move with and through my fragile, damaged body and spirit, to heal. He also helped by laughing, playing, and talking with me, as soon as I was able. Within a year, we felt lifted by love as we "danced"—skiing together down mountain slopes.

Joan's skilled touch,[5] given through daily massages in the rehab unit followed by frequent massages when I first returned home, also helped my aching body. This touch reminded me of her professional massages before my accident, of my full athletic body, and of our unique friendship as she provided generous, loving care to help me move beyond current pains.

Friends who are professional colleagues also sorted out the complex needs of my clients: communicating with all of them, doing interim therapy for those who could not wait for my return, remaining On Call for me while I was not working, communicating with my office landlord, sorting and bringing mail to me. Later they gave free consultation to help me return to work, and they helped transition clients back to me.

Colleagues who are also close friends suggested a gathering in my home:

"Why don't we have a dinner and invite the women who helped you logistically or spiritually in your healing and preparation for returning to work? This could include people who worked with your clients, gave you consultations, prayed, visualized, or in some other way helped you. We could have a drumming circle, share stories, and have a ritual ceremony to demarcate your return to work and to affirm your pursuit of full healing," suggested Dana[6] who first conceived this gathering.

"Fantastic idea. I'll help plan this," said Margaret[7] who had been On Call for me that fateful day.

During our evening together, everyone shared her personal story of hearing about my accident, then subsequent involvement in helping me—and Nicole. Words of love and wisdom were expressed. We had a powerful circle of drumming. Then all together laid their hands on my head and body as they voiced healing and success wishes for my return to work and my full life. We ended by sharing food prepared by Dana and me, along with laughing together at absurdities.

Before we parted that September evening, I said, "Thank you all, from the bottom of my heart. You've given me the love, support, and courage to recover and return to work. I'm such a fortunate woman, to be here now, to be here with you. I will carry your stories and energy with me while I'm back in my office and work. Namaste."

Return to work celebration at home with Nicole and colleagues.

Then they spontaneously encircled me as a group while each gestured with hands together and said, "Namaste" (meaning *I bow to you*).

I cannot emphasize too strongly how profoundly the reactions and reflections of others matter in healing. I felt this time and time again, after my big accident. I hear and see this every day in my office. I encourage family, friends, and mental and physical healthcare providers to be vigilant about what is felt, said, and done around recovering people. As Rachel Naomi Remen wrote: "The heart … may be far more powerful a source of healing than the mind."[8]

On the opposite end of experience, a few friends and family said and did hurtful things after my accident. I am choosing now not to recount these stories; they really do not deserve focused attention or time. Shocking? Yes. Controlling? Yes. Self-interested? Yes. Mean? Yes. True friends? No.

Some others whom I had imagined might come forward to help me seemed to almost disappear. Years later I heard why, with apology:

"I was coping with the shock of cancer and radiation. I didn't want to burden you with that on top of all you were going through. But I had no time or energy to help you or Nicole."

"My sister suffered an irreversible severe head injury from an accident, and she became mentally incompetent. That happened shortly before your accident. I couldn't deal with the news of your head injury. It was all too much, too scary."

As often happens in life, the disappearance of these friends, for example, was about them, their traumas, and not about mine. Thanks to open, heart-felt conversation, these relationships eventually got reset.

My experience of God's love and spiritual presence provided transcendent, uplifting love. As explained before (Chapter 14), after my big accident I was stuck in a painful anxiety state for several months. Alternative and somatic treatments helped me tune in to memories and feelings related to my accident. This helped me experience in my body the sensations and emotions of being still here[9]—the miracle of my survival. I was then able to put all subsequent stresses in a different perspective: I am alive for many reasons, including to mother Nicole, to do my work, and even to share my experience through writing this book. It was not yet time for me to die, or I would have. I really should have, given the accident. And when it is time to die, that will be OK, too.

I see the Oneness of all in an entirely new way. But this is not a book on spiritual attunement. It is a book about falling down, surviving, and reviving. Nevertheless, the peace and love of God provided huge energy and support beneath my broken head and wings.

My experiences of love from some healthcare professionals, clients, colleagues, friends, family, and God provided a lifeline in my journey beyond trauma. In many ways we really are simple, as The Beatles sang to the world in 1967: *All You Need Is Love.*[10]

The United States medical system is the most expensive in the world. It absorbs 17.6% of the gross domestic product, twice the average for developed countries. Yet in healthcare statistics, such as life expectancy and infant mortality, it ranks near the bottom. Carole's experience with it after her accident shows us, more vividly than any statistics, what is wrong with our medical system, and why we pay so much for so little.

Insurance is based on the concept of distributing risk, to help people survive loss of health, family, or property. Its history goes back to ancient times. But most insurance companies today (as Carole found out) are organized to maximize profits and minimize service, making it as hard as possible for policy holders to collect.

Carole learned that the medical industry has changed for the worse since she worked as an RN. It has become increasingly fragmented, with specialists who often do not communicate with each other and order tests that may be botched or misunderstood without doing a full patient assessment. Moreover, much of the published research on which specialists rely is flawed, as shown by the meta-analysis of Dr. John P. A. Ioannidis,[1] Professor of Health Research and Policy at Stanford School of Medicine. Carole also learned how bureaucratized and top-heavy hospitals have become, with patient care no longer controlled by those who provide it.

Since I develop and teach courses in wilderness and pre-hospital emergency care, my students learn low-tech methods, starting with traditional patient assessment. This requires them to communicate with and empower patients – skills that have become rare in medicine, as Carole learned from her experiences. Fortunately, she had the knowledge and will power to protect herself and regain her life; and in this chapter she shares what she has learned about dealing with medical and insurance bureaucracies as a patient after her accident.

(Reflection by friend Steve Donelan,[2] www.wildernessemergencycare.com, 2014.)

19

NAVIGATING INSTITUTIONAL MAZES

My head even now swims as I contemplate this topic. Institutions can be huge, complicated and difficult to navigate, like mazes. Go forward. Get stuck. Back up. Try again. And try again.

I have already described the maze of the Bay Area hospital for inpatient rehabilitation, imbedded in the larger U.S. healthcare delivery system that is a much larger maze. As our high tech medicine becomes more and more expensive, our healthcare is also being taken out of the hands of providers, so that patients must deal with labyrinthine bureaucracies and giant corporations.[3] There are no simple solutions here, as evidenced by continuing political debate, rising fears with financial stresses, and a large aging cohort of our population. How can we promote healing of individuals while we navigate huge, complicated institutions?

From my experiences in healing, both of myself and in my work as a helping professional, I believe that Integrative Medicine[4]—incorporating Western/Allopathic and Eastern/Alternative/Complementary Medicines—is important, that neither Western nor Complementary Medicine is enough by itself. Western Medicine is good at surgery, healing acute illnesses and infections, and high tech diagnostics. Complementary Medicine is good at building immunity, promoting health, disease prevention, and balancing alignment of the body as well as energy. Integrative Medicine combines both approaches and is being taught more regularly in healthcare education programs. Consider utilizing the best of Western and Complementary Medicine.

I chose not to look in the mirror often after my accident, as this gave me reflections of the trauma of hitting that tree. Instead I coped by receiving reflected love from close family and friends, by remembering and visualizing my full self before the accident, by tuning inside my current body-mind-emotions-spirit, and by looking out so I could remember to see others and the world beyond myself. Upon returning home, I took on receiving Integrative/Holistic support of my healing as a halftime job: I sought and found excellent specialists in both Western and Complementary Medicine.

After my discharge from the Bay Area hospital for inpatient rehabilitation, I was forced to deal with other, nonmedical institutions. My health insurance was a huge problem. Craig at first volunteered to sort out my medical bills: to ascertain what they were for, when they needed to be paid; to question charges that did not make sense; and to challenge nonpayment of those charges that should have been covered by my insurance policy. I was happy to let go of this as the stack of medical bills quickly grew to nearly two feet high. I knew I had purchased one of the best private health insurance policies available to individual families in California back in 2000, one that let me seek and choose specialists as needed.

After several months of multiple phone calls with customer service agents who worked for this insurance company, a different agent answering each call, all promising to clarify or resolve some discrepancy or confusion with no results, Craig threw up his arms in exasperation. He could no longer tolerate trying to slog through the mess of documents created by my healthcare providers' billing companies and by my health insurance company. By then I was no longer as anxious and agitated as I had been since I hit that tree, and I could tolerate dealing with my health insurance. So, I thanked

Craig for his efforts and took on the paperwork of my healthcare morass within one of the largest health insurance companies in the U.S.

I wrote out lists: provider name, date of service, amount paid by my insurance, deductible owed, co-insurance owed. I put associated bills behind each list. Then I methodically started calling my insurance company about denied and unprocessed claims as well as providers about where my insurance company was in their payment process. This went on and on for several months, with few resolutions, beyond those things that had been easily billed by and paid to providers. Then I asked to speak to insurance claim agent supervisors. But personnel changed frequently, even at the supervisory level.

No one at the insurance company would assume accountability for my complex healthcare insurance case. Health insurance companies should pay medically necessary bills without delay. Yet some bills were paid while others were not, with no apparent pattern.

After some months, healthcare institutions and some providers started threatening to attach my still-owed claims to the equity in my house if I did not pay the bills immediately. In total exasperation, I called the California Department of Insurance to file a complaint against my insurance company. Through this department, I learned valuable information that now saves time and the hassle of useless repetitive phone calls to insurance customer service agents.

I want to share this hard-earned knowledge with you. To challenge insurance nonpayment, file a "grievance" within your insurance company. Each insurance company has forms, prepaid envelopes to a unique grievance address, and responds with an intelligent written answer within 30 days after receipt of the complaint. If you believe something should be paid and the insurance company has deemed it as "not medically necessary," get a letter from your doctor explaining why it was medically necessary, and send this along with a grievance form.

Before I learned about the grievance process—and insurance companies often do not disclose this process unless directly asked—it was as if I were banging my head against the wall when I tried to resolve disputes. Now, whenever I disagree with denial of payment, I file a grievance. This is not a waste of time; it is a relatively simple process, much less time consuming than being put on hold on the telephone or wading through pages and pages of data on the Internet. Either I get a clear explanation about the limits of my policy and why no payment was made because of that, or a decision is reversed and I am paid. If still not satisfied, the procedure then is to appeal the denial, and finally to send a formal written complaint to the Department of Insurance in the state where you buy your insurance policy.

With validation of "medical necessity" by my doctors and the grievance procedure within my insurance company, I was able to get my health insurance company to pay over $20,000 of medicals bills that they tried to shift to me. As a psychologist and healthcare provider, I have gotten insurance companies to pay what they authorized in writing prior to treatment and later tried to deny, by naming the law being violated and voicing my intent to report them to the Department of Insurance if they would not pay.

We are not as powerless as insurance companies would have us feel, and challenging them is relatively simple once you understand the process:

1. Get your M.D. to write a letter of medical necessity if required.
2. File a grievance if the charge is denied when it should have been paid.
3. File an appeal if grievance does not work to get your payment or to adequately clarify why there was no payment (it rarely gets to the appeal stage).

4. File a formal complaint with the Health Insurance Department/Commission in the state where your policy resides. (I have never had to do this; the state will not look at a complaint unless you already have gone through at least the grievance/appeal process.)

Knowing this process would have saved us hours and hours of phone calls, being on hold, being given no helpful answers, feeling financially threatened and overwhelmed. It is satisfying to get a timely, intelligent, written response to an insurance problem; and filing a grievance is a way to make that happen.

Most recently, with problems related to health insurance changes in the U.S., I have learned that it can be particularly helpful to find a good private insurance agency for dealing with your insurance needs and the healthcare system. I always had managed my healthcare insurance directly with the company. I now have an excellent agency[5] (see Notes and Resources, if you are interested), and this has saved me hours of aggravation in the past few years; it also has quickly gotten me the best policy for the best price with the best company, which can change with each calendar year.

As a last resort, and unfortunately occurring more and more frequently due to corporate greed, there is always the Class Action Lawsuit route against insurance companies. I personally have benefitted from this when such a lawsuit was instigated by other persons battling my health insurance company.

Another huge institution I had to deal with was the DMV (Department of Motor Vehicles, in California). I was told at the inpatient rehab unit that I could no longer drive because of my head injury, and that this had been reported to the DMV. When I felt ready to drive again, several months after hospitalization, I was returning to work and my doctors were in agreement that it was now safe for me to drive. So I casually called the DMV to ask about their process in reinstating my driver's license. That was a big mistake.

I learned the hard way that with the DMV in California, it is best to assume your driver's license is OK unless you receive written notice of suspension, revocation, or probation. Asking the question of how to reinstate my license generated a complicated process that only then threatened my license. Apparently, the in-patient rehab unit staff had never reported my head injury to the DMV, or it had somehow fallen between the cracks in one of these two institutions. After calling the DMV, I was required to: write a letter of explanation; provide letters of mental and visual driving ability from doctors; provide detailed vision and field of vision test results obtained through special instruments and tests done at an ophthalmologist's office; wait until all this had been processed at DMV; and then take written, visual, and driving exams. Then I was granted a license on probation, requiring medical approval every six months and no traffic violations or at-fault accidents for several years. I was required to pass a written and visual test with each license renewal for fourteen years after my accident. All of this would have been avoided if I had known that my license was still valid so long as the DMV did not tell me otherwise. Fifteen years later, I am grateful to finally again be offered a simple, standard driver's license renewal process.

Another institution I had to deal with was my private disability insurance company through my work. I knew I had purchased some kind of income protection but I did not fully understand how my disability policy worked. Over time I learned that I would be paid nothing until after 90 days of disability, and if I had any earnings, I had to claim partial disability and provide monthly business income and expense statements plus corroborating reports from my primary care doctor along with written self-reports every three to six months. Because I have a private practice as a psychologist, money trickled in from client insurance claims during the time of my hospitalization, which was part of the actual time of my complete disability. I returned to work part time, and I gradually learned how the disability insurance payments were calculated and how best to deal with my company in order to receive payments legitimately due to me. Navigating this maze took attention to details and mathematical abilities. An accountant could also have done this job, but I needed to keep expenses as low as possible because of my decreased income. Also, I believed it was good to exercise my brain by doing the math myself.

In time, the disability company started pressuring me to accept a "buyout settlement" of my policy. This process is similar to that with car insurance: let us pay you a set amount and you give up all future claims, i.e. to this accident with car insurance or to this policy with disability insurance. In the end, I agreed to a buyout settlement, for the sake of peace and health. I did this long after my disability insurance company first wanted me to: I waited until I was emotionally ready and until doing so fit with the financial advice of my tax attorney.[6] Because of this buyout, I no longer have disability insurance, beyond that available at the federal level (SSDI). And because of the severity of my accident, I am not insurable. For this reason, I waited until my late 50s to agree to the buyout settlement. My private disability insurance would no longer be payable after age 65 anyway.

I also had to learn how to navigate institutions related to care of the elderly, because my mom was incapacitated by dementia and just after my hospital rehab unit discharge, I received papers with the notice that I was now her sole executor and guardian. When I called for help to make sense of the paperwork, my mom's trusted Elder Law Attorney, Helen Hempel,[7] explained, "Your mom's paperwork probably got lost in the institutional system after your stepdad died, until you were identified as your mom's remaining executor."

After sorting through the papers I sent her, Helen called: "This is all more complicated because you didn't receive these papers until now, five months after your stepdad died. It took me a number of hours—and all my legal knowledge—to sort everything out. It was a mess not only because Severt (my stepdad) couldn't deal with it as he was dying but also because the legal system was slow and the paperwork got piled up."

Helen explained the Elder Care Laws in Oregon to me and sent the now organized and understandable paperwork back to me. I used the finances still available to help my mom and also to help my siblings visit her the last two years of her life. Gerontologist doctors taught me a lot about the end-stage process of my mom's Alzheimer's. I was grateful to have the help of the attorney and healthcare professionals in this complex institutional maze of nursing homes, Medicare, Medicaid, and Elder Care Laws in Oregon, where my mom and some other family members lived.

As adults, we often need to take on helping our parents as they age while we are also helping our children who are growing up. This stage of life has aptly been called the "Sandwich Generation," and all these demands can add to the number of institutional mazes that often need to be navigated after an accident or other trauma. It is good to have help along this complicated path—to seek it, ask for it, and accept it, as needed.

Our goal in Taos Ski Valley is to play with the challenges of the extreme and beautiful mountain terrain here: in charge and in control, to allow our relaxed minds and bodies to move and perform with confidence, grace, strength, and balance. That is the motivation and attitude for the performance of modern skiing.

We teach more advanced skiers than most other resorts, giving them respect as athletes. We also learn from the elite of the world competitive athletes, coaches and instructors. Taos has been acclaimed as the #1 ski school in the U.S. for: our attitude, passion, and shared enthusiasm for the sport; our constant search for new feelings and emotions as we savor our beloved mountains; our love for the snow and the elements, whatever the condition—with no hesitation we are willing to explore and thread the thin line on the edge of the latest skiing techniques.

There is a unique mood, spirit, and identity here. We share the magic of Taos with our guests, and they feel like part of our family.

Carole, you are one of my inspirations, for all the turns we share together. You: right on the tail of my skis, attacking exuberantly, with a big smile. I love your gusto for life, and it is no surprise to me that you came back to the mountains, to express in movement and action your passion and loves. I apply myself to be in shape mentally and with my body as well. I never want to disappoint you when you return to the snow.

Love, Jean[1]

(Reflection about his love of mountains, skiing, Taos, and about my return to the mountains after my accident; by Jean Mayer, Technical Director of Taos Ski School, my ski mentor and friend, September 2014.)

20

FACING THE MOUNTAIN

Mountains have deep and nearly lifelong meaning for me. As early as age eight, I enjoyed climbing mountains. I have a memory of camping with my family in the national forest outside Bend, Oregon, our hometown. I was proud of myself for climbing to the summit of Broken Top Mountain with my dad, whereas the rest of the family tired out or lost interest. I loved the beauty and the challenge. The same was true for skiing, which I began at age 12.

But after slamming into that tree in a ski race, the memory of trauma in my body changed my unabated love of mountains. Many people might have chosen to never ski or climb again after enduring such an ordeal. I heard such comments as:

"Life in the city is far safer than what you endured while you were 'having fun' in the mountains."

"If you ever try to ski again, you are insane. Why would you do that? You already tempted fate once. You have a daughter. Are you really going to ski again? How crazy could a person be? Is this your idea of fun?"

"Carole, you've already used up your nine lives. Give it up so you can enjoy what's left. You're lucky to have anything left."

But people who know me well understood that it was natural and expectable for me to want to ski and climb again. They understood my deep love of being in the mountains: soaking in the natural beauty and delighting in the exhilaration, thrill, and mastery of being an expert skier and of climbing challenging mountains.

What kind of a nutter was I? Just another thrill-seeking, adrenalin junky, trying to prove something to myself? As I pondered these challenges from others, my mind flashed back across the many mountain experiences in my life.

Skiing was my adolescent rebellion, my way of forging independence. It gave me time to enjoy myself away from my parents after my family was wracked by the pains of divorce. Sharing my love of skiing also deepened connections with my brothers and with others, eventually leading to love, partnership, and the birth of precious Nicole.

Bend, Oregon, had only 13,500 people in 1964. Mt. Bachelor Ski Area was less than half an hour away from Bend and had only a day lodge back then. I'd heard about skiing through other kids at school and asked: "Mom, my friends at school tell me how great it is to ski. Can I learn to ski?"

"Sure, Sweetheart. But you'll have to earn the money to pay for it yourself, because I'm financially stretched as far as I can go."

"OK," I replied.

In 7th grade, I talked my oldest brother Ed[2] into driving and going skiing with me. I supported my new interest with money earned by washing windows, ironing, and babysitting; this money allowed me to rent gear and buy the $5 day lift tickets. Ed and I had a lot of laughs and fun as we skied. This athletic time together provided a new dimension to our relationship as we shared those days of skiing.

I loved skiing from the first moment I put my gear on and headed out. I was a natural. Being relatively poor, I could not afford lessons. So I watched others, mimicked those I thought looked skilled. Being a teenage kid with my own measure of testosterone,

I crashed and burned until I learned how to turn and stop on the bunny slope by the rope tow. This took only a few days.

By the end of that first winter of skiing, I was hooked and wanted to earn more money so I could go up to the mountains every weekend. I also really needed separate time from family demands. I was, unknown to myself at that age, trying to separate and individuate. Skiing became my ticket for that.

At the end of 7th grade, at age 13, I found a summer job in Central Oregon: picking green beans a bit, strawberries a lot, and living in a dorm for working teenage girls. Highly motivated, I became a fast strawberry picker and earned at least $1.50 an hour, well over the minimum wage for teenagers in Oregon back then.

By the time school started in 8th grade, I had enough money to buy a full set of ski gear and a season pass. I felt proud of myself for working so hard and earning this. The winter of 8th grade, when Ed in 12th grade was often too busy to ski, my mom dropped me off at the ski hitchhikers sign at the edge of town. Nice families picked me up there and drove me to and from Mt. Bachelor. I was always among the first on the mountain and last to leave when the slopes closed. I did not want to miss a minute of this new, self-earned thrill, so I skied all day and ate my lunch on the drive home. By the end of my first full winter of skiing with season pass and my own gear, I skied parallel turns well on all the slopes at Mt. Bachelor. And I absolutely loved to ski.

The summer I turned 15, my mom had remarried and the blended family had moved to Europe, where she and my stepdad worked in international education. In 10th grade, I fell in love with Austria when I first skied the Alps on a school trip. I began dreaming of taking a year off to teach skiing in Austria after high school, so I studied German as my foreign language. By 11th grade, our family had moved from Holland to Norway, which had some decent skiing.

On winter weekends, my younger brother Dave[3] and I took

the bus from Stavanger to Madla, stayed in dorms there, and skied our hearts out. We also had some family trips to Sinnes and Geilo during school vacations, thanks to my mom and stepdad. Dave and I skied at every opportunity, even when the lifts were closed and we had to hike up the runs, even in the rain. We were a bit touched, and we grew closer as we shared these adventures.

Early October of my 12th grade in Stavanger, Norway, I received a letter from Rudy Studer of Crans-Montana, a French speaking area in the Swiss Alps. Rudy owned the International Summer Camp Montana,[4] which was then called La Moubra Sports Center in the winter. He had gotten my name from the superintendent of the high school where I had attended 10th grade in The Hague, Netherlands. Rudy had been assured that I was an intelligent, hard-working, English speaking young woman—just what he needed. His letter concluded: "Would you please come work for me? By the way, I need for you to begin by the end of October."

As I read this letter, I felt astounded and flattered. I laughed out loud and said to my mom, "Nice offer, but wrong language and wrong year." I had my focus on Austria, not Switzerland; I was studying German, not French; and I was a serious student.

My mom's response shocked me even more than Rudy's letter had. She was my English and history teacher, plus the vice principal of the small American International High School in Stavanger. She had two graduate degrees and valued education. Yet, seeing that I was under-challenged and under-stimulated by my small peer group there (U.S. kids of North Sea oil drillers), my wise mother said something I never would have imagined: "Oh, high school, shmigh school. You can always go to high school. But when do you get an opportunity like this? Go for it!"

"You're kidding?"

"You've always done extra work in school. With a little bit of correspondence effort after ski season, you'll probably be able to graduate this school year anyway. Go, and have a wonderful time!"

So, with the blessings and encouragement of my educator mom and stepdad (director and principal of my high school), I became a high school drop out. At the ripe old age of 17, I left home for good. I flew from Norway to Geneva, caught a train to Sierre in the Canton Valais, and was greeted by large flakes of light snow falling gently from the sky as I was met by the Studer family. This was all arranged by letters and faith. There were no cell phones, faxes, or Internet in those days, and international calls cost a fortune.

I consequently spent the majority of my senior year of high school skiing and working. And I did graduate anyway, by spending merely three weeks in May doing correspondence lessons to complete my required courses. I learned to speak passable French because I had to, though I'd never studied it. Quite naturally, I learned more by working, traveling, and being independent that year than I ever would have learned in classes at the Stavanger American High School.

I spent two winters, springs, and summers in Switzerland and had many adventures. But that is another story. By the time I left and decided to return to college full-time in the U.S., not just autumns as a student at an international college in Luxembourg, I had immersed myself in Alpine skiing. In Montana-Crans, I taught private ski lessons in the winter, skied with male instructors in a Swiss ski promo movie, and directed the glacier skiing program for Rudy's International Summer Camp. While heading the summer camp skiing program at International Summer Camp Montana, I flew in glacier planes with campers—from Sion to the foot of the Matterhorn above Zermatt. We skied by the Matterhorn once every few weeks in the summer. This was stunningly beautiful. Then we took the cable car down to Zermatt, had a picnic, caught the cog-wheel train for an hour ride to Visp, and were picked up by the International Summer Camp van.

I also worked as bar tender and then secretary at La Moubra during the non-camp seasons. During the summers, I had worked as head counselor in charge of 10 staff who worked and played with 100 campers ages 5 to 10, then as assistant camp director. My two years in Switzerland were full and expansive. I loved living in the Alps.

Through living and traveling much in Europe in the late 1960s and early 70s, I was able to see a far larger world than I had experienced as a poor kid in Oregon. By being a "ski bum" in Switzerland, I expanded my mountain abilities, work abilities, and comfort with new people and encounters. Thus skiing had become a strong part of my enjoyment of life and sense of mastery in the world. Skiing had helped me to separate and individuate from my family of origin. It had given me a separate sense of self as well as an independent life, at quite a young age. I felt grateful for all of these childhood and teenage experiences, including my early years in Oregon.

By the time of my big accident in 2000, I as an adult had enjoyed many skiing, mountaineering, professional, and personal adventures.

I not only had taught skiing and been a high school dropout and ski bum in Switzerland, I also had lived in Vail, Colorado, 1975-76 (working as a nurse and skiing almost daily); developed a network of ski buddies in Colorado and Lake Tahoe; skied most of the great resorts in the Western U.S.; bought a cabin in the national forest near Lake Tahoe, California, to facilitate my passion for skiing while being a mother[5] and family woman; skied over three million vertical feet of helicopter-accessed deep snow on the steep slopes in trees and wilderness mountains of British Columbia,[6] Canada; and developed a friendship with Jean Mayer—zen master of ski instruction—in Taos, New Mexico, who became my ski mentor. By this time of my life, I was in the habit of skiing as many days a year as I was years old: a hard feat for an aging professional who works in the city, but it seemed only right that the older we get, the more fun we should be able to have.

I had climbed Mr. Rainier, Washington, by two technical routes, Bugaboo Spire in B.C., The Matterhorn in Switzerland, many other mountains in Colorado, Wyoming, California, Washington, and three of the big volcanoes in Mexico. I had skied the Haute Route[7] in Switzerland with friends. I also had climbed to 21,000 ft. in the first all women's climbing expedition in China's history, attempting to summit Mt. Kongur[8] in the Pamir Himalayas.

People who knew me well understood that I was careful when needed. For instance, I had been the first climber above advanced base camp who decided to turn around on the Himalayan expedition in 1986; then the other three women high up on Mt. Kongur at that time decided to retreat with me. All in our group made it home alive during what proved to be a treacherous, snow-filled, death-filled season of Himalayan climbing. I considered that a success, though we were all disappointed not to reach the summit.

When I returned to skiing after my accident, I learned first-hand about PTSD: Posttraumatic stress disorder, coined after the return home of many traumatized Vietnam War veterans. PTSD is a type of anxiety disorder following extreme trauma that involves the threat of injury or death. I treated people with PTSD in my work as a psychologist. It was quite another thing to live in it and work through it.

I considered myself quite lucky in the timing of my injury: I missed no ski days. Skiers are odd and think like this. My accident happened the last day of the 1999-2000 ski season, and by November of 2000 I was back at work, running again, and physically ready to give skiing a try. The first ski runs at Lake Tahoe were opening then.

Fortunately, I have a sense of humor and I understood the classic physiologic response to trauma. Craig, Nicole, and I decided to ski a half day on Thanksgiving at Heavenly Valley, CA, where artificial snow often makes for some of the best early season skiing at Lake Tahoe. We planned to meet my friend Donna who had invited us to Thanksgiving dinner later in the day with her family.

Despite my knowledge of PTSD, I was astounded by my body's response to putting on ski boots in the parking lot. My heart rate escalated, and I had a feeling of panic that washed over my body. As a means of coping, I joked about myself with Craig and Nicole as we all prepared to ski: "Oh no. I'm going to have a heart attack walking across this dry, paved parking lot." Laughter together and the acknowledgement of my fear helped. Then I reminded myself out loud: "Actually, Carole, you could ski a beginner run blind."

I quietly, internally, continued to reassure myself: *Your body is kinesthetically well-trained in this simple athletic endeavor. This is quite different from ski racing, because you get to choose where to turn. Relax, honey. You're going to be OK.*

While Nicole stood guarding our skis, Craig and I went to get our tickets. I shared with him the strength of my PTSD experience, not wanting this to scare Nicole, yet feeling the need for his support. He suggested: "Why don't we start on beginner runs, and you follow me down the first run? I can be your seeing eye dog."

Given my continued visual difficulties, I happily replied: "Great plan. Thank you."

Craig's plan worked well, and by the end of the second run, my trauma reaction and heart rate had calmed down. We all then breathed a sigh of relief, had another good laugh, moved on to intermediate runs, and had a fun half-day of skiing together again. We earned that yummy Thanksgiving dinner, and I felt like I spent more calories with the PTSD than with the skiing itself.

Skiing with Nicole at Lake Tahoe before accident.

Skiing and joking around with Nicole at Lake Tahoe after accident.

I then started preparing my muscles and psyche to return to heli-skiing in the Monashees, in British Columbia: to go with a group of friends in January that I had skied with every year since the 1980s. I noticed that injury to the nerves surrounding my right eye gave me double vision in all but the downgaze at that time. Also, because one eye tracked like a still camera and one like a moving camera, this hindered my depth perception and made me dizzy and disoriented. Skiing easy terrain resulted in double vision: two bumps, two trees, for each, etc. Skiing in steep terrain resulted in single vision. Hooray! Steep skiing was my favorite anyway, and I could see correctly, when there was adequate light.

The Monashees are famous among powder hounds for steep and deep powder tree skiing. Skiing there is like none other. I was excited to return … and a bit scared. I mused: *What if I have a PTSD freak out in the wilderness? What if my agility and strength are no longer good enough?*

Nicole was freaking out, weeping, screaming, and begging me to stay home: "Mom, how could you do this to me? *Pleeeeeeeaze don't go. You'll die.* I'm *really, really* afraid you'll die. I'll never forgive you."

I knew I had to go, for my healing process. I did not want that hideous ski accident to restrict my life or Nicole's life. Nicole had seen me go heli-skiing every year of her life, even had gone to Canada with me when she was young.

I hugged and held Nicole, as I did my best to reassure her: "I will be careful, Sweetheart. I promise. Remember: I've been heli-skiing every year of your life, with no problems. It's different from ski racing; I get to choose where to turn, so I can be safe. I'll call you every morning before you go to school and after skiing every day. And I'll take you heli-skiing when you finish high school, as a special 'job well done' treat; then you can experience how special it is to do this kind of wilderness powder skiing. We'll probably go to the Bugaboos, a really cool and beautiful place."

Nicole continued, with sobs: "I know you love it but it's not worth the risk. I'll do anything for you if you cancel your trip. Why don't you just give it up, Mom? You're lucky to be alive, and I need my Mommy. PLEASE, PLEASE, PLEASE don't go. I'll hate you and never forgive you if you go. How could you do this to me?" etc. Nicole has a strong personality and did not back off her pleading.

Thankfully, Craig had offered to stay home with Nicole, to support her and my going to the Monashees. When it was finally time for Nicole to leave for school on the morning I was going to fly to Canada, she pulled a Gum Shoe on the sidewalk in front of our home: she put her arms and legs around my legs and used all the body strength she could muster, trying to physically hold me down, in Berkeley. It took the strength of Craig and of me to make Nicole let go. I held her again as she wept, promising, "I will call you as soon as I arrive safely in Canada." We did get Nicole to school, and she was reasonably OK emotionally by the time I hugged and kissed her goodbye, reminding her I would be calling frequently.

Later that morning, Craig took me to San Francisco International Airport, hugged me, and with tears said, "Be safe."

I responded, also with tears: "I will. And thank you so very much for all your help and for being you."

When I was on the bus between Calgary and the Monashees, I told my "tree buddy" (we pair up heli-skiing for safety): "Richard, I totally understand if you want a different tree buddy this year. I've skied to prepare for this, but you can see from my appearance that I was badly injured. I plan to be cautious and imagine I will not fly down the mountains as usual."

I was surprised by Richard's kind response: "I want to ski with you, and I know you'll ski well. Certainly you won't ski slower than the year I went to Hawaii and hadn't skied at all before our Monashees week."

Up at the Monashees Lodge, north of Revelstoke in British

Columbia, Roger Laurilla,[9] mountain guide and manager there, greeted me with a big hug: "I'm so glad you're alive and back at CMH (Canadian Mountain Holidays), Carole."

"Thank you, Roger. That means the world to me."

When Roger was free, I went into his office and had a brief, private chat with him: "I think I'm ready to do this, but I'm also a bit concerned about how I will actually manage skiing in this demanding terrain. But then I reminded myself, I could always ski with Fred" (the then 79 year old Austrian American intrepid leader of our group of 44 heli-skiing friends). Fred, a fabulous man and athlete, was slowing down with age.

Roger nodded with agreement. Then he added: "Carole, I'll give you a private guide if you need it, to help you return to heli-skiing, so you can go faster than Fred and without the pressure of keeping up with a group."

"Roger, I'm deeply touched by your offer and generous spirit. Wow. Thank you."

Then Roger and I agreed that I would start out in my usual group with Richard as tree buddy, since Richard had offered, and change my guiding needs as dictated by my skiing. Such amazing support from these tough athletes.

Returning to heli-skiing in the Monashees was indeed a critical experience in my healing process. Within two days, I was skiing as always there, flying through the deep powder between the trees, enjoying taking small jumps as dictated by the terrain, feeling the exhilaration of landing in light and puffy powder, once again feeling like a bird floating down through this winter forest. Once again I was in heaven. The trees did not scare me. I felt strong. And my vision worked well in the steep terrain. I had my expansive ski self back again. Hooray! And I felt more gratitude than ever here in the Monashees. No PTSD here.

Heli-skiing on Elevator in Monashees, B.C., Canada, 1980s, before accident.

Heli-skiing on Big Red in Monashees, B.C., Canada, 2011, after accident. Photo by Roger Laurilla.

Fourteen years later, my tree buddy Richard told me: "That first winter in 2001 you didn't have your usual instinctive sense of direction; so, I had to carefully make certain you didn't get separated from the group." Now that is the mark of a great tree buddy when heli-skiing: he without comment helped me out. That problem of disorientation matched the visual spatial losses that were seen on my neuropsych testing. Fortunately, these improved over time.

I called Nicole twice a day, and she and Craig did well in Berkeley. We were all happy to reunite ten days later. My going to the Monashees had been a healing experience for them, too. I knew that I really needed to go. The outcome was even better than I had imagined, and I felt it down to my bones.

I enjoyed the rest of the 2001 ski season and was amazed when Jean Mayer, Ski School Technical Director and instructor of the top ski class in Taos Ski Valley, New Mexico, invited me once again to ski in his class, despite my accident and vision issues. Jean had called and written to encourage me over the summer: "Get well, and believe you can heal. I know you will be back in Taos and back in my ski class this winter. You can do it." Jean had even put a photo of my skiing with him on his St. Bernard Hotel website.

Jean is a remarkable man, extraordinarily generous, and a true master of ski instruction. He is also infectiously fun, filled with joie de vivre. The week of skiing with Jean for my birthday, in 2001, my ninth year in a row there, also tremendously helped my healing process. I received excellent technical instruction on groomed runs and then followed right behind Jean as he went down steep and demanding bump runs. It was easier for me to follow Jean than to pick my own routes because of my challenged vision. Yes, I had fallen down—in a big way. And I had the good fortune of being able to get up and return to skiing and the mountains I love, to share these experiences with people I trust and love.

It was not surprising when Joan[10]—my friend, massage therapist, Himalayan climbing buddy—and I decided to climb Mont

Blanc, the highest peak in the European Alps, in June of 2001. We both had wanted to climb this majestic mountain. Bad weather before our ski tour had foiled my plan to climb Mont Blanc in 1987, when I had been in Chamonix, France, and skied the Haute Route with friends to Zermatt, Switzerland. Joan and I had separately, on different years and with different friends, traversed the Alps from France to Switzerland on mountaineering skis. Yet Mont Blanc still beckoned us.

What better way to commemorate my survival and recovery from my big ski accident?

Joan planned our route: the Gouter, a classic route up Mont Blanc. As we began our climb, I was surprised to find that I again experienced PTSD while doing the rock scramble on the lower aspect of the ridge. "I thought I was over that," I explained to Joan, who could see the fear on my face along with my careful, tentative movements. I could see that Joan was worried about my PTSD, wondering if it would impede our planned climb. Neither of us discussed this further until after we returned home.

Bad weather slowed us down for a few days after we ascended the lower rock ridge. We waited for good weather at the Gouter mountain hut, just beneath the glaciers and more technical aspect of the climb. This gave me time to work with myself mentally and emotionally, so that I gradually acclimated to mountaineering again and could focus on the task at hand.

Joan and I successfully reached the summit of Mont Blanc on June 30, 2001, a year and six weeks after that fateful crash into the tree. Fantastic! We were thrilled. It was a long and exhausting climb; it was also a clear, sunny, and beautiful day on the roof of the Alps. How do you recover from a trauma? One step at a time. Even if the trauma and recovery are big. Just as Mont Blanc is.

My full self was back. I had returned to work well. Then I needed to return in this embodied, mountain-loving way. Some people thought I was insane, truly out of my mind. I was merely attempting, in the best way I knew, to tap into my inner strength and reclaim my body and my life. I believe that we each must find our ways to recover from trauma.

... And I did take Nicole heli-skiing in the Bugaboos when she was 18. She was the most natural, skilled first time heli-skier I ever saw in my four and a half million vertical feet of skiing wilderness powder in British Columbia.

In all my time as a skiing safety consultant, of the many hundreds of people I've known who decided to sue a ski resort, the vast majority did so not out of any desire to get rich, but because they wanted to make a difference. They wanted to see improved safety so that what happened to them won't happen to anyone else. Carole is a sparkling example of this.

Virtually all skiers wrongly assume that there are broad safety standards for the slopes and trails that are enforced to reduce unnecessary and hidden risks that could hurt them or their children. They are incredulous when they or a family member is seriously injured, and they learn too late that there are no such standards at all—none. As Carole once did, all their lives they bought into the myth perpetrated by the ski industry: it is in the business's best interest to do everything possible to make sure customers have safe and enjoyable experiences, also that the Forest Service and CalOSHA[1] *are the watchdogs for public safety. It's what we would all expect, and it seems right.*

CalOSHA does require that certain standards be met for chairlifts, but not for the slopes and trails. The Forest Service has neither the money nor the mandate to monitor safety on the slopes and trails of their permittee resorts. They are absentee landlords at best— nothing more. And as far as ski resorts are concerned, it's all about the bottom line. Ski resorts are big business nowadays and are owned and run by powerful conglomerates. They have used their power and wealth over and over to hire lawyers and lobbyists to promote protective legislation and to prevent laws that would mandate safety improvements.

These facts have been well hidden for years, but it is my hope that Carole's decision to write about her experience may bring the myth to light and begin to empower the skiing public to decide to choose their resort, at least in part, based on its safety record.[2] *Our children and our brothers and sisters are too important to leave safety to the whims of the powerful ski industry. "It can't happen to me if I just pay attention to where I'm going" is a wrong-headed attitude that puts you and your children at risk. It can and does, all the time. Carole's experience proves that. Read Carole's story: hopefully with more knowledge and activism, it will not one day be your story.*

(Reflection written by snow safety expert, Dick Penniman,[3] November 2014.)

21

Resetting the Course

When my life was reset by that fateful ski race—even with my focused, dogged determination to reclaim my life—I also came to understand that the ski racecourse had been set improperly. Given that no one else had survived such an accident as mine while ski racing and that my life had miraculously been spared, I felt called to do what I could to help improve ski racing safety. I wanted to help prevent others from unnecessarily enduring the kind of trauma I had experienced.

In the summer and fall of 2000, as ski friends from Colorado, New Mexico, British Columbia, Oregon, California, Nevada, and Utah called to see if I was OK, to offer condolences, and to try to figure out what had happened, the facts of the ski racecourse gradually were clarified. One heli-ski friend, who has a successful ski-racing daughter, posed the largest number of concerned questions. Friends' questions included:

"You're such a good skier. How could this have happened?"

"Ski races should always have safety gates. Weren't there safety gates?"

"How far was the racecourse from the trees?"

"Ski racecourses should always be put in the center of a run, with fences top to bottom, for the safety of the racers. Wasn't the ski run closed to the public to ensure safety for racers?"

"This whole thing sounds really bad. You should *not* have had this experience and should not have to be going through this nightmare. Have you sought legal counsel?"

I had never considered such questions. I was an expert free skier but naïve about racing. I had trusted my daughter's ski racing team coaches—who set up the course—with Nicole's life as well as my own. When friends asked these questions, I began to think and understand more about ski racing—too late for my own safety, but not too late to take a stand for the safety of others.

I was advised to contact Dick Penniman[4] of Truckee, California, who was a ski safety expert. Dick was friendly and explained fall zones in ski racing to me: "The way ski racing gates are set up dictates the ski turns. Each turn has a specific centrifugal force related to where it is in the ski racecourse. So the G-forces around ski gates dictate where the expectable fall zones will be. Fall zones are the predictable force and direction of fall if an error is made turning around each ski gate. The safety of the racecourse should be set up with this in mind, because in ski racing there is no choice about where to turn for the sake of safety. In racing, the goal is speed around the gates, not safety. So the ski gates with their attendant fall zones should be set up with adequate distance from obstacles including lifts, trees, and other skiers. Safety gates should be placed for protection from falling into any hard obstacles, including ski lift towers and trees. All ski teams and coaches should be trained in and follow these procedures. Setting a racecourse up on the side of a run in order to keep the run open to the general public on the other side, with gates as close as 10 to 15 feet from trees in the fall zones along with no safety gates, should never be done."

"Whoa. Thanks for explaining this to me. This is news to me, and it really helps me understand what ski friends have been trying to explain." Then I thought further to myself: *If I had known about fall zones and safety gates, I would absolutely have refused that Family*

Fun Relay Race for myself and forbidden it for Nicole. I was so ignorant and trusted her ski team.

Dick Penniman was a former ski patroller and patrol supervisor in the North Tahoe area. He is concerned about snow and avalanche safety; by the late 1970s, Dick was the go-to expert in this area. I had been referred to the right person.

In a later conversation when Dick and I were discussing how his knowledge and defense of ski safety had changed the course of his career, he shared: "During the Star Wars years, people protecting the ski industry started calling me Darth Vader. I said, 'I think you have this backwards. The ski resort industry is "The Empire" here. I'd compare myself more to Hans Solo.'"

We both laughed, and I agreed.

Dick Penniman is now the Chief Research Officer with SnowSport Safety Foundation[5] in California, a nonprofit organization established in 2008, to improve snow-sport safety and injury prevention. I am so glad that Dick has taken a strong and courageous stand for ski safety in California. The SnowSport Safety Foundation was established after my "Resetting the Course" legal ordeal following my accident.

Meanwhile, when the ski team head coach called to ask how I was doing the summer of 2000 (a kind gesture), we had an intense dialogue:

"It's been a really rough time," I said.

"I saw you in Reno and even with all the bandages, you looked beautiful there," he replied.

I almost choked hearing his words, because I had heard quite the opposite from all others: I looked terrifying, scary. Rather than engage in a useless argument about my appearance, I decided to cut to the chase: "Why was the racecourse set so close to trees and without safety gates?"

"We don't have the money or manpower to put safety gates up from the top to the bottom of a race."

"It would be better to have no race than an unsafe race. That is true for team practices and racing, as well as any family races," I replied.

"Look, we're trying to be supportive of you. We're having a fundraiser to try to help you out financially, and we'll give Nicole a free year of racing with us next winter and you a free season ski pass. We're so sorry you had this accident."

"Look, I'm concerned about safety for ski racers at the resort. I appreciate your kind offers, but I need to know that you will set up safe racecourses in the future, complete with safety gates top to bottom as they are at the regional championships in Mammoth, with adequate protection in the fall zones," I responded, still focused on the bigger picture.

"We can't afford that," he said.

"Then you need to do fundraising to facilitate safe ski racing, not fundraising for me."

Silence. … Finally he said, "I was just calling you to reach out in support."

"I appreciate your doing this. And you need to know that I'm dead serious about this concern; well, nearly dead. If I don't see a change toward providing safe ski racecourses at your resort this coming winter, I'll seek counsel and pursue this legally. I don't want what happened to me to happen to any young racers, or their family or friends."

I was hoping to see a positive change the next winter, but I did not. As Ron Wecht,[6] the attorney who took my case, later said to me: "The coach was between a rock and a hard place. If he changed the race safety there, he would have been admitting fault. If he did not, he had to contend with you. Either way, he could lose, and he knew it."

"But he should have known me well enough after four years to trust that my goal was safe ski racing for the team, not a legal battle."

"That would require a lot of trust, which apparently wasn't there," Ron replied.

The first summer after my big ski accident, I received phone calls from many attorneys, who apparently had heard about my accident. Legal action was not in my mind; survival, healing, and returning to work were.

Dick Penniman had referred me to Ron Wecht, a personal injury attorney in San Francisco who is an expert on legal issues of ski injuries. I learned a lot through this experience about safe ski racing, good and bad attorneys, and the value of seeking excellent legal help when needed.

When I first met Ron for a consultation the fall of 2000, he explained in detail the legal process I could expect: "The statute of limitations for this is one year, so if you decide to initiate a lawsuit, it has to be done before April 16, 2001. Alpine County, where this ski area is located, is a very tough and conservative county legally. This lawsuit could take five to seven years. It could be complex and costly, so you should not do it with the anticipation of becoming wealthy."

I trusted Dick's referral to Ron, and I liked Ron's professional style, so I said, "I want to see what the ski area does with their racecourses this winter, to give them a chance to change. If I decide to pursue this legally, would you be willing to represent me?"

After careful consideration for about a week, Ron called: "I believe that you and your situation deserve good legal counsel, plus it would be a challenging and interesting case for me, and I think we could win. However, you need to understand that what is right and fair is not always what wins in court. It will be a risk, for me with regard to time and expense, for you with regard to time and emotions. If a similar lawsuit were to occur in San Francisco, a very good settlement would be offered in short order, with no need to go to trial. In Alpine County, we might have to endure a jury trial and perhaps appeal it."

I liked Ron's intelligent, straightforward, no-nonsense legal approach, and I felt comfortable working with him. Because Ron had explained the statute of limitations for this situation, I knew I could legally afford to wait, watch, and hope for a change in ski racecourse safety for the team during the season of 2000-2001.

When no racecourse changes had been made that winter, I contacted Ron in March 2001 to initiate the legal process. I felt both sad and determined about doing this. I learned a lot about attorneys and lawsuits, because a settlement was not reached until May 2006.

First, the ski resort's insurance defense attorneys responded by filing a demurrer, a "so what" legal document that objected to the lawsuit as irrelevant and illegal because I had signed the team's liability waiver. It is ironic because that waiver was written for parents to sign for kids, so we all had joked the morning of the race: "Right, I am really my parent, signing for my kid self. And," we said sarcastically, "this racecourse is really dangerous, risking life and limb on that intermediate run."

Ron had to go to court in Markleeville to protest the demurrer, and he lost. He next appealed in Sacramento and won. Then we were back to square one.

There were months and years of discovery, the pre-trial phase of the lawsuit that included evidence sought by both sides. I had to spend huge amounts of time digging deep into my memory and all of my written and financial records, providing facts, witnesses, medical records, bills, etc.

When it felt like too much time and energy were required to cope with this lawsuit, I reminded myself of my goal: to help make ski racing safer. I reminded myself of my good fortune in actually being alive, able to do this. I coped with nasty snubs from some Tahoe ski buddies who disagreed with what I was doing. I got a few minor stress-induced illnesses from lack of sleep and had to learn to pace myself, to prioritize the many demands on my time and body. After the depositions, some members of my family had strong emotional sequelae—their own delayed PTSDs—that were challenging for all of us. This lawsuit really took its toll on us, yet it still felt important to us all. My family thankfully was in absolute agreement with my choice to take legal action. I kept my vision on the goals of safety and justice.

Ron explained to me in 2000: "There are only two major insurance companies representing the ski industry in the U.S. They will do anything possible to win and keep things as is, regardless of safety. There are no regulatory systems or statutes for ski area safety in California."

Dick later explained: "The ski industry is regulated in every way except for racecourses, trail safety, marking hazards, those kinds of direct skier safety issues on the slopes. Defense attorneys protect against that, ostensibly to protect the resorts, yet they make money on lawsuits. So this is both complicated and self-serving."

I learned from Ron that ski safety only becomes mandated as a result of lawsuits and costs after accidents. Having skied 36 years before my 2000 accident, I was astonished to learn this truth. Incredible. So I was now engaging in this backwards system. Unlike the state health insurance commission, there was no ski area safety commission to which I could appeal and provide pressure for a change in racecourse safety at the resort where my daughter was involved. However, because there were only two insurance companies, if a settlement with me hurt them financially, it could potentially have a ripple effect in ski race safety across the country, with the insurance companies wanting to avoid future similar legal problems and costs. Also, a victory in court could set a precedent and change case law on ski safety. The system seemed strange to me. But Ron and I worked within it, and I focused on my goal of helping to establish some kind of ski race safety standards.

We had a settlement negotiation conference in Sacramento for a theoretical attempt to curtail a court trial. The judge at this settlement conference saw that the ski resort's defense team had no intent to settle and said in private to Ron and me at the end of the day: "They offered such a lowball figure that they clearly were not making a good faith attempt to settle. They wasted my time and yours. A whole day. Unbelievable."

We saw that they were trying to wear down my attorney and me, to waste our time and money, probably hoping we would just give it up and go home. They did not know with whom they were messing. Ron and I both have sturdy minds and characters. Ron had been a fighter pilot in the military: "We learned to stay focused until the mission was complete, and we landed as safely as possible."

So, we prepared to go to jury trial in Markleeville, California. I had a thorough neuropsychological assessment again, which was mentally and emotionally tough on me. I had a full physiatrist/rehab doctor exam and evaluation.[7] Both of these were in preparation for expert witnesses in court. All this faced me squarely in the eye with my physical losses from the big ski accident. Even with my focused intent on reclaiming my life, I was not whole, not 100% back in every way. Though I was aware of this before, it was painful to be shown my deficits in such detail. Meanwhile, my family was coping with emotional trauma in two members, triggered by the depositions and seemingly unending lawsuit: an adolescent acting out and an adult in deep depression.

In the end, less than a week before our jury selection and trial was to begin, the ski resort defense team finally offered a reasonable settlement. Ron explained: "The settlement expense to them is large enough to make the impact you wanted on ski racecourse safety, even though they would not in writing agree to set safe ski racecourse standards as part of the settlement offer, which you had requested. Though very low for San Francisco as well as low given the many costs of this lawsuit over five years, the settlement is enough to cover legal and medical costs incurred by the lawsuit, and will partially pay for your lost income and still occurring medical bills. I advise you to accept the settlement, unless you emotionally need to have your Day in Court, to voice your position in a recorded public venue. Some people do need and want to do that. Another factor is that a jury trial would be in Alpine County, and depending on the jury, I could lose in court, because they are very protective of the ski industry. Then, even if we won an appeal in Sacramento later, you would likely not receive more money because of increased costs of the lawsuit, and it would take a toll on your emotions and time."

I appreciated Ron's direct, sage advice and responded: "Given all that, I'll happily agree to settle, to finally let this process go. Thank you for years of hard and intelligent work on my behalf, for your belief in defending me, not giving up, and your helpful influence and impact toward the setting of more safe ski racecourses. I've so appreciated your clear communications about the legal processes, expectations, and risks with such a lawsuit. You've given me a whole new impression of lawyers, good lawyers. WE DID IT!!! And I'm very relieved to finally be finished, to not have to go on with our trial date."

We did make an impact toward ski racecourse safety, the biggest we could, given the system at that time. Because Ron had always been clear with me about what I could realistically expect, I had not anticipated wealth from this lawsuit. No amount of money could have made up for that accident, anyway.

The ski resort and ski education foundation (ski teams) wanted me to sign an agreement that I would never disclose the amount of settlement paid nor the fact that we had settled or any other details of this lawsuit and settlement. I agreed to never disclose the settlement amount, and I have kept that agreement. I refused to sign the gag request for no disclosure that there had been a settlement at all, though I knew my refusal might lead to a tough trial. I was a bit surprised—as was Ron—and very pleased that they settled anyway. I knew I would want to disclose and write about this, to help further ski racecourse awareness and safety.

In our situation, Nicole[8] legally could have had her own personal injury lawsuit with her ski team and resort—anytime before age 19, nine years after she quit racing with the team—for the injury my accident had caused her. Ron told me about this during our work together on my lawsuit, and I let Nicole know. Nicole considered it, discussed it in detail with me, and consulted with Ron about it when she was 18.

I was relieved when Nicole chose not to pursue a ski injury lawsuit herself. We had already made an impact on ski racecourse safety through financial pressure. We had watched the team gradually change and set up safer racecourses. Nicole had lost her desire to ski race after that Family Fun Relay Race of April 16, 2000, but we still enjoyed recreational skiing together. I was glad Nicole chose to focus on her life now, on moving forward, rather than dredging up the past.

I also am writing about this arduous lawsuit to share with you a few important facts that I have learned. If you think you might need legal help, get a good referral and have an initial consultation early, so you know your legal time limits (statute of limitations) and what is involved. Choose an intelligent, hard-working attorney who is a good communicator and has a track record of successful experience in your area of concern. Assess whether the arduous nature of the legal process is really worth it to you, if you are willing to spend much time and have the physical as well as emotional endurance to see it through.

But life holds mystery for us yet. In a hundred places
we can still sense the source: a play of pure powers
that—when you feel it—brings you to your knees.

There are yet words that come near the unsayable,
and, from crumbling stones, a new music
to make a sacred dwelling in a place we cannot own.[1]

(*In Praise of Mortality, Selections from Rainer Maria Rilke*, Translated and Edited by Anita Barrows and Joanna Macy, 2005, 115.)

The most beautiful thing we can experience is the mysterious. It is the source of all true art and science.[2]

(*Living Philosophies: A Series of Intimate Credos*, by Albert Einstein, 1931.)

Your very survival was God's mercy and grace. I was impressed with your surgeon who prevented further problems from swelling and loss of blood. Your recovery was miraculous. It was a total miracle—and you have continued to make contributions in life. Your functioning has far surpassed reasonable expectations and reasonable hope.

(2012 reflection by my brother Jim,[3] who came to Reno the day after my accident.)

22

Mystery and Miracles

I consider it a miracle that I am alive today. My story is complicated, as numinous experiences often are. It blows my mind (no pun intended) when I ponder the multiple intertwining experiences that eventually got revealed after my accident. As I write while sitting in my bedroom rocking chair, I notice a lovely picture showing the hands of an elderly woman weaving a native basket in a circular pattern that contains the superscript: "Weaving the stories of our lives...." This picture has hung in my bedroom for over thirty years, and the longer I live, the more I am moved by the truth of this image.

It just so happened that Toby Rowland-Jones,[4] a first responder from Big Sur, was skiing with the Hawthorne[5] (racing/artist) family the day of my big accident. Toby had stopped to watch me race, and then he saved my life in that tree well.

It just so happened that April is a time of bald eagle migration in the Sierra Nevada Mountains. Dixie,[6] an animal researcher and a shamanic friend of my friend Margaret[7] (who was On Call for me at the time of my accident), did a shamanic[8] healing journey on my behalf when she heard about my accident. Dixie later shared that during her journey for me, she saw a spirit eagle who had intervened to cushion and soften the blow as I hit that tree with my head, without a helmet at high speed. Very interesting given that few people have ever survived a skier versus tree accident, none before while ski racing. Very interesting, also, because eagle[9] became one of my power animals when eagle first visually came to me during hypnotherapy sessions with Maggie Phillips[10] in the late 1980s. Eagle later came again to me in real life, flying above, as I journeyed on and later led Vision/Wilderness Fast retreats[11] in New Mexico and in the Sierra Nevada Mountains of California during the 1990s. Dixie had no knowledge of that.

At the same time that Margaret and Dixie were doing shamanic journeys on my behalf, I later learned that many individuals and groups across the country and internationally were praying,[12] lighting candles, visualizing, and chanting for my survival and recovery. There was a large interfaith group sending spiritual help my way.

It just so happened that Jay Morgan,[13] a neurosurgeon and a spiritual man (currently the Chief of Neurosurgery), was On Call at Washoe Medical Center in Reno the Sunday afternoon I had my big accident. After carefully examining me and ordering needed CT scans to help plan what was needed through surgery, Dr. Morgan spent over three hours meticulously, surgically removing blood clots, then piecing back together skull fractures and a large laceration, so my brain and head could heal. He and the trauma staff[14] saved my life.

When I called Dr. Morgan in July after my April accident to thank him for his excellent surgery and medical care, to let him know I was beginning to work, jog, and resume my full life, his response was a simple and humble: "Thanks be to God."

Then the next ski season it just so happened that a friendly ophthalmologist[15] was sitting across the dining table from me, as guests eat family style at the Hotel St. Bernard[16] in Taos Ski Valley, New Mexico. I was there enjoying my annual birthday ski trip. At this point, my right eyelid would only open half way, and I had double vision for the most part. This certainly added a whole new dimension to bump skiing.

Observant, Martyn looked at my eye and asked, "What happened to your right eye? An accident?"

"Yes," I replied, and then briefly told him about my accident.

"Has anyone checked you out for a blowout fracture of your right eye orbit?" he inquired further.

I summarized my eye saga for Martyn: "My neurosurgeon in Reno suggested this be done as soon as possible because of fractures seen on my CT scans. When I saw ophthalmology specialists back in the Bay Area and asked about a blowout fracture and repair, I was told that was not my problem: 'Your right eye will probably never open properly again. It looks like you crushed your third cranial nerve, so your eyelid will not open and your eye muscle will not look up.' Yet, meanwhile, a neuro-ophthalmologist confirmed that my optic (visual) nerve was intact and functioned well, even though my eyelid was completely closed. So I tried many alternative treatments that helped my eyelid open this far."

After dinner, Martyn asked, "Would you mind if I briefly examine your eye?"

"Please do." I marveled at his helpfulness and attunement.

After carefully checking the mobility of my right eyelid and eye muscles, Martyn offered to help me: "I'm going to contact one of my teachers at the excellent Wilmer Eye Institute[17] at Johns Hopkins in Baltimore, Maryland, to see who would be the best surgeon for you, if you're willing to travel."

"Absolutely. I'd be happy to travel or do anything to get my eye and vision correctly fixed."

Then another friendly and intelligent couple who had joined the visit at our dinner table added, "We live in Baltimore, and we'd be happy to help you with this, too. We have connections at the hospital, and you're welcome to stay with us."

I was awestruck by this turn of events over dinner in Taos, grateful for this unrequested help. I had tried unsuccessfully to pursue the concern of a blowout fracture with many ophthalmologists all over the greater Bay Area.

Martyn was true to his word. He took my email address and phone number. Within a month, Martyn called to let me know that he was referred to Allen Putterman,[18] a specialized eye surgeon in Chicago. He added, "Chicago is a lot closer to California than Baltimore, so I imagine this would be OK for you?"

"Oh yes. Can you give me his contact information?"

"I can call Dr. Putterman to speed up this referral for you," Martyn offered.

"Wonderful. Thank you so much for all your time and help, Martyn. I really can't thank you enough."

"Well, you're a fellow skier, and I want you to get totally well. I'm happy to do this."

Martyn then called Dr. Putterman who told him, "I could see her, but it would make more sense for her to see Stuart Seiff[19] in San Francisco, closer to Berkeley and easier for follow-up. He's an excellent surgeon, did specialized occuplastic training at the Jules Stein Eye Institute at UCLA and then did further post-residency training at Moorfields Eye Hospital in London. He should be able to assess her situation and know the right surgery without any oversight."

Martyn immediately contacted me to share this good news. I contacted Dr. Seiff's office and was given his first available appointment. This was just over a year after my ski accident. Within days I was called about a cancelled surgery, so I did not have to wait for months. Dr. Seiff examined me, ordered new CT scans, and we both had to scramble to get everything ready within a few more days for my first eye surgery. This was the blowout orbit fracture repair that should have been done three to six weeks after that fateful ski race; at least it was finally done 13 months after my accident, thanks to the miracle of sitting across the dinner table from Martyn in Taos Ski Valley.

Also, it just so happened that a few years before my ski accident, friend and colleague Marcia Black[20] had seen Maggie Phillips for hypnotherapy—referred by me following Marcia's car accident. Maggie had then suggested that Marcia join her to attend a workshop, focused on somatic (body) healing of trauma, that Maggie taught with Peter Levine[21] at Esalen Institute.[22] Peter had developed a new specialized treatment approach and training program: Somatic Experiencing® (SE™).

In response to Peter's work with Marcia during that workshop at Esalen, a year after my accident Marcia decided to begin SE™ training herself and invited me to join her: "This is amazing work, very different from psychotherapy, well worth learning. I'd love to share this time and experience with you. Want to apply and join me?"

I felt very tempted, but I knew that I still needed to focus on my own healing, as well as earn money to pay all my bills. "It's just too soon after my accident. I really wish I could, but I know it would be too much for me now," I replied with regret.

Marcia's SE™ knowledge then led to my daughter Nicole's first SE™ treatment a year and a half after my accident, with Ariel Giarretto.[23] Ariel had just moved to the greater Bay Area, after years of working at Esalen and teaching around the world with Peter.

It just so happened that nearly five years after my accident, I felt healed enough to be able to learn SE™, to add this somatically based skill to my practice as a psychologist. In many ways, SE™ training was a natural progression for me, based on my pre-psychologist R.N. training and work as well as now on my increased interest in trauma recovery. Meanwhile, Ariel decided to teach SE™ to experienced body therapists and psychotherapists in the Bay Area. Having met me before, she knew that I had wanted to join Marcia's SE™ training class. Ariel called me the fall of 2004, with her unexpected and perfectly timed invitation: "I'm going to start a specialized SE™ training group for experienced therapists in January. I'd love to have you join us for this training. Can you?"

"Fantastic. I hope so. What dates?"

I was concerned about starting SE™ training not long after Nicole started 9th grade at Berkeley High School. I knew that parents need to be around, to stay tuned in to what teens are doing in high school, so I thought to myself: *Perhaps I should wait until she leaves for college, or at least until she's well settled in high school.* I then discussed my opportunity with Nicole and our family.

Nicole's response surprised and reassured me: "Mom, go for it. We can be studying together, and you'll finish about the same time I do. You can graduate from SE™ when I graduate from high school."

I called Ariel back and happily said, "Yes, I can do it."

Adding Somatic Experiencing® to my professional repertoire proved to be a gift in my personal and work life.

Shortly after beginning SE™ training, during the late spring five years after my accident, it just so happened that the third and seventh cranial nerve regeneration to my right eye had finally plateaued. So it was time for strabismus (eye muscle) and ptosis (eyelid) surgeries,[24] to complete my aberrant but nonetheless remarkable nerve regeneration as much as possible with the help of highly skilled and specialized eye surgeons.

In the process of my three year training to become a Certified Somatic Experiencing® Practitioner (SEP), I learned that the curriculum requires classes, supervision of practice, and receiving treatment sessions as a client. I reasoned within: *What better time to receive somatic sessions than now, to help with my eye surgeries?* Unlike psychotherapy, there was no conflict of interest within SE™ for having sessions with my teacher.

SE™ treatment can be done via talking or touch (along with some talking); Ariel was trained in both. I had chosen mostly hands-on alternative treatments for healing the trauma in my body caused by my ski accident, so it was natural for me to choose hands-on as well as verbal treatment with Ariel.

As Ariel gently put her hands onto my head, to help prepare me somatically for my eye surgeries, I was surprised to go back instantly and experientially into the tree well, the site of my ski accident. This was my second flashback, my first since the CST flashback with Cathy Adachi,[25] nearly five years before.

"I just went back to the tree well where I hit the tree."

In her skilled SE™ approach, Ariel gently queried, "Who found you? When was the first time you knew you were OK?"

I mentally scanned my situation in the tree well and replied, "Yes, I *am* OK."

My eyes were closed, focused on this flashback, yet intuitively I felt that Ariel was surprised by my response. With eyes still closed, I scanned my situation and said: "Wait a minute. You lived around Esalen and Big Sur for years. Perhaps you know the man who supported me and saved my life in that tree well. His name is Toby Rowland-Jones."

Now I could feel that Ariel was stunned. There was silence. "Toby was my former partner; we were together for years, and I used to do some first responder work at accidents with him around Big Sur."

"You've got to be kidding. For real?"

"For real."

Ariel and I were both absolutely astounded. Chance? I think not. Mystery? Yes. Toby had never before skied at the resort where I crashed into the tree while ski racing. He was there and saved my life. I gave Marcia a referral after her accident, and that ultimately led to our both being trained in SE™. Through my daughter's trauma from trauma needs, I got to Ariel who was now my teacher and knew Toby well. The web of all our lives was interwoven. I was spared, I am alive, I got to finish raising my daughter, and I have things to share, through the profound web of healing and loving people in my life, through all our work, and through this book.

The web continues, the weaving of the fabric of life. It just so happened that Ariel went on vacation about the time I had eye surgery, so I was only able to have a few SE™ sessions with her in preparation for my eye surgeries. Ariel then referred me to Kathy Kain,[26] touch specialist in SE™, who had agreed to see me post-op in Ariel's absence. This felt full circle as I had initially tried to have my daughter see Kathy, when Nicole needed somatic treatment a year and a half after my accident. Kathy's practice is always full, with people on her waiting list, so Kathy had referred Nicole to Ariel. Now I was Kathy's client.

Kathy later was one of my Advanced Level (third year) SE™ instructors, along with Steve Hoskinson.[27] This Advanced SE™ training was brilliant and challenging. I took a year of post-SEP Touch Skills Training for Trauma Therapists from Kathy. The Touch Training felt like an even bigger full circle in my professional life: back to my hands-on work as a nurse, with the addition of 30+ years training and experience as a psychologist, plus the recent training in somatic treatment of trauma (SEP), after I had gone through a near death experience. I feel blessed by these four years of education that provided two SE™ certifications.

Many mysteries, miracles, synchronicities, full circle experiences, and further weavings in the web of life. Since "dying," after initial severe panic, anxiety, fear, sadness, and anger, I have eventually come to feel deeply in my body that "all is well and all shall be well,"[28] even when I am upset emotionally about some specific challenge, even with intermittent personal, family, friend, and world chaos. I know from experience, from the inside, that much happens beyond my understanding, though some things eventually do get revealed.[29]

"God, grant me the serenity to accept the things I cannot change; the courage to change the things I can; and the wisdom to know the difference." This timeless "Serenity Prayer,"[1] *brought to public awareness by theologian Reinhold Niebuhr and now intoned by millions daily in twelve-step meetings around the globe, was daily fare for me as a twelve-stepper. But it was Carole's practical application of it that brought the prayer to life for me when we worked together as nurses in an inpatient alcohol and drug treatment program during the 1970s. "Make three columns on a piece of paper: cannot change, can change, need wisdom," she had instructed our patients. "Then as different issues in your life arise, write each in the column where it seems to fit, and you will find greater clarity." I have done so since.*

And who among us does not claw our way toward acceptance? Or ask: "What distinguishes true acceptance from mere tolerance or lifeless resignation?" "What rightly clamors incessantly for the appearance of acceptance's sister, true hope, and not for the siren call of counterfeit wishful thinking?" For me each hard-wrested moment of acceptance has not come from a linear progression but has ebbed and flowed like the tide, crashed at points in another tsunami of grief, or settled with gently lapping waves.

Being deeply at peace with and truly finding gift in what is, rather than what might have been or what is wished for, evokes a deeper, truer yearning and beckons us forward. When acceptance does take gentle root, its blossom is gratitude. I am grateful and honored to have shared the journey toward acceptance with Carole. One of the affirmations we have for encouraging one another shimmers in my being each day: "The way it is . . . it is enough."

(Reflection by Sandi John,[2] friend and colleague, 2014.)

23

Acceptance

Acceptance is a complex, nuanced, and often a confusing beast. I use the word beast rather than process because of how hard I had to wrestle with it as part of my own healing journey. Coming to acceptance was very painful yet also felt freeing when I finally got there. In response to trauma or illness, acceptance can emerge with different individualized decisions: to seek further possibilities for healing, to accept less than full healing as the best possible outcome, or to accept movement toward death. It can also be a potentially unnecessary acquiescence toward death. Acceptance is a very personal decision, to be made by the individual coping with trauma or illness; or, for a person incapable of making or expressing that decision, by someone who knows and loves them.

As I ponder my own acceptance journey, friends Gerry and Nancy come to mind. They as a couple lived through extreme examples of the complexities and gradations of acceptance. Gerry[3] and his family have given me permission to share their remarkable stories with you.

While Gerry recounted his and Nancy's stories, we discussed in great detail his memories of their illnesses. Gerry's memory of the sequence of events of his own near death illness following surgery was totally absent for the first six weeks after his hospital admission, then somewhat unclear. This kind of memory confusion is a natural response to many medications as well as to severe trauma.

As we talked, Gerry became curious about the details, wanting to piece together a coherent whole understanding. He then read medical records, Nancy's journals, and talked with his five adult children and their spouses to sort it all out. Gerry found this process of sorting, sharing, and understanding to be deeply healing, as did I.

Gerry would not be alive today if his wife Nancy had not believed that Gerry would recover. After surgery to replace two heart valves on August 15, 2000, while recovering well, Gerry needed a second surgery for some internal bleeding. After the second surgery, Gerry's respiratory system completely shut down in a medical condition called ARDS (Acute Respiratory Distress Syndrome). This occurred a week after his initial successful valve surgery. Gerry was then in an apparent coma (unresponsive, possibly paralyzed) and was put on a ventilator. He developed a condition that appeared to be corticosteroid-induced myopathy: Gerry had a loss of muscle tone and feelings up to the top of his neck. Corticosteroids are often given to patients while on ventilators, aimed at helping them get off ventilators faster. Doctors involved were not willing to discuss with Nancy the potential involvement of steroids in Gerry's muscle weakness.

By a month after his first surgery, Gerry had developed kidney and liver failure; kidney dialysis did not help because his blood was clotting in the machine. In addition, Gerry did not respond to the doctors' standard neurological stimuli and physical exam tests. Two neurologists gave Nancy and their children the impression that Gerry was "brain dead" (though they had not taken a standard EEG to assess brain wave functioning). Two other doctors wanted the family to unplug Gerry and allow him to die, because of "multiple organ failure" (heart, lungs, and kidneys).

One doctor met with the family and said, "Let him go—stop everything, give morphine."

Gerry's doctors and other medical caregivers said, "We don't think it's worth trying to keep Gerry's body going. We do *not* expect Gerry to survive, and if he does survive he will be a vegetable."

That day a social worker joined the family in the cafeteria, and said, "You're being cruel to Gerry to keep him on life support."

Meanwhile, Nancy, along with their children, plus Gerry's brother and a prayer group, all saw: "Life. Gerry in the Light. Gerry is holding on." Nancy noticed that Gerry was responsive with his eyelids. He was able to blink his eyelids or not in response to her saying: "Gerry, blink," then "Gerry, don't blink." His brain was alive, but Gerry could only move his eyelids to respond. Nancy, and then all their children came to see and know that Gerry was responding to them with his eyes.

Nancy was eventually able to convince a doctor to sit with her so she could show him Gerry's eyes' responsiveness. He saw and then agreed not to give up on trying to keep Gerry alive. But without the family's attunement to Gerry and their intervention, the doctors would have neglected to do a thorough assessment and would have stopped all life support and allowed him to die.

Within a day of his family being told to "let Gerry go," Gerry was able to nod his head. The next day Gerry moved his thumb, and the next day he moved his toes. Four days after his medical crisis when it was assumed by staff that Gerry was going to die, he was able to spend three hours breathing without his ventilator. By six weeks after his first surgery, it was found that Gerry's heart and valves were functioning excellently. From then on Gerry's recovery seemed assured, despite several blood transfusions, bouts with pneumonia, and other setbacks.

Gerry is very alive and well today. His road to recovery was long and arduous, given that almost all his systems had shut down. Their children drove Nancy back and forth to the hospital when

Gerry was in ICU. Then Nancy stayed in the hospital with Gerry until his discharge, protecting his life, providing love and care. Nancy slept in several hard chairs put together until she found a small folding cot. Gerry healed enough to begin regaining his memory in early October. His loss of conscious memory was likely due to drugs, as Gerry was later told that he spoke many times before his first memory (similar to my experience in Reno, while on morphine).

When Gerry started remembering things, he was aware that his family was there; then he worried about money, insurance, and the approach of his 65th birthday. Gerry's feeding tube was removed in early November. Because of repetitive pneumonias, Gerry was kept on a ventilator from which he was slowly weaned between late November and early December. Gerry was happy to be discharged home from the hospital on December 15, 2000, four months after his admission and heart valve surgery. Gerry then first walked at home in mid-January, was able to negotiate stairs by mid-February, and felt more normal by March. He healed quickly after he could walk (as did I), and he healed much faster after leaving the hospital and returning home. PT and rehab took six months at home.

At age 79 (October 10, 2014) Gerry lives independently in his house with many stairs in the Berkeley hills. He loves tending his vegetable garden, being with family and friends, going for long walks, enjoying music, theatre, good food, and active involvement in life. Gerry has deep gratitude that Nancy did not accept the doctors' pronouncements that he would not survive.

Gerry now lives alone because his wife Nancy died. Nancy first had a hysterectomy in November 2005 to remove two cancers in her uterus. The hysterectomy for cancer removal was followed by chemotherapy because of cancer in a few lymph nodes.

When Nancy's cancer metastasized, she knew that she would not recover. A routine surveillance lung x-ray in December 2006 showed spots. Biopsy of lung spots and CT scan were done January

2007. Because Nancy's and Gerry's 50th wedding anniversary was February 1, Nancy decided to wait until after their celebration to see her oncologist and make medical decisions.

The metastatic cancer was found to be the one (of her original two) that was very aggressive, poorly responsive to any chemotherapy, and was most likely to metastasize to lungs. Fortunately, the cancer originally found in Nancy's lymph nodes had been the one that could respond well to chemotherapy. Now Nancy suddenly had hundreds of inoperable small cancer spots in her lungs. Chemotherapy might delay death by a few weeks or months, or maybe not. The toxicity of chemotherapy would make it a miserable experience. With no young, dependent children at home, Nancy, with Gerry's support, felt there was no need to put herself through such torture.

Nancy wanted to spend her last months feeling as well as possible, to be present for her loved ones and to die consciously with acceptance. She did try some nontoxic alternative treatments but did not want to be wiped out by drugs that would not save her life.

In the end, Nancy had to sit up in order to breathe. First she sat at the kitchen table. She loved to cook and share her bounty with others, so this was a natural place for her to sit and feel good. At the very end, Nancy sat on the edge of her bed, resting her head on a pillow on a table. Through all this, Nancy emanated light and love as she said, "I'm not afraid of dying, but I'm sad I have to leave the party early."

Nancy died at home, just a few months after diagnosis of her cancer metastases, aged 69. All her family and a few close friends were with her on her last day. Nancy shared a deep, loving glance with each and said, "You sweet, sweet people." She stayed alive until her last child arrived, her daughter Helen from Spain. Nancy died very consciously, with no mind-altering drugs, no pain (as lungs have no nerves that sense pain), but struggling mightily to be able to get a breath. Nancy was supported emotionally by loved ones who gathered to her side, physically by family and close friends who took turns helping to support her head, and spiritually by her trust in God. Nancy showed, in an exemplary way, that there is a deep light in each of us that needs space to shine as long as we are alive, even in the process of dying.

Both Gerry's and Nancy's stories are of acceptance, though with opposite outcomes. I have profound respect and amazement at Nancy's unflinching courage that was shown in her paths of acceptance both for Gerry and for herself.

If I had gone along with the story told to me, and told about me to my family, friends, and colleagues by some "rehabilitation" staff in Reno and in the Bay Area, I could now be living in a setting for brain injured people incapable of independent life. I would not be writing this book or continuing my private practice as a psychologist. I would also not be engaged in life with my loved ones, jogging an hour four to five days a week, much less enjoying a myriad of interests or seeking more ways to deepen spiritually and to give back because of the gift given to me of continued life.

I knew that the brain injured nonfunctional geek story was not mine to live out. I am grateful that Dr. Morgan[4] worked so well during his neurosurgery on April 16, 2000, believing I would recover, that some of my loved ones still saw me for who I really was and am, saw the fire in my eyes and understood that I just needed time, love, and help to recover my life.

On the other hand, after I had completed healing from my last two right eye surgeries, I had to accept some deficits, losses that I could not recover. I wanted everything back, my entire life as before. But after seven years I slowly came to realize that I needed to accept where I was in the present. Endless and varied complementary/alternative treatments in addition to excellent Western medicine and further eye surgeries would not help me get everything back. I had recovered far more than I was told was possible given my injuries, but I would not be made *100% whole* in my body.

I really did need to accept that the physical healing would not be perfect, that I had done all I could, and it was time to let go of trying new things, time to accept. This was hard for me. It required an existential shift with regard to my healing. I had been hell-bent on healing fully. Now I needed to accept partial healing as good enough. The kings, with all their horses and personnel, did put Humpty, me, back together again. Yet, I still had a few cracks and small holes (metaphorically speaking). Thankfully, I believed in holistic healing long before my accident, not just on the physical plane but also on the spiritual dimension, what Deepak Chopra[5] has called the "holiness of healing." Despite my lack of full physical healing, I needed and wanted to affirm my current state of health, to experience myself as spiritually whole, perhaps even more so than before my trauma.

Physically, I went from appearing attractive and young for my age, with symmetrical features, physical strength, and wild flowing long curly hair to appearing very much my age, with somewhat asymmetrical eye muscles and lids (even more so when I am tired, and in addition my eye asymmetry is gradually worsening with the sagging muscles of age), plus being more vulnerable physically, along with wimpy ratty hair (and most recently a loss of hair near the scars on my head).

My visual-spatial acuity is not what it used to be. I still have to deal with double vision sometimes, including the impact of that on my depth perception and balance. This adds a whole new dimension to risk of falling as I age.

Though I have recovered in a remarkable way, able to work and enjoy life, the neuropsychological assessments that were required several years after hospitalization for my lawsuit and for my disability insurance, as well as the medical evaluation for my lawsuit, drove home what I knew to be true but chose not to give focused attention. My brain, though working well enough to reclaim my pre-accident life in many ways, is not functioning as well as it was.

On the other hand, I am aging, now 64 rather than 48. Learning new things is harder for me, takes some repetition. My short-term memory is less keen, so I take many notes to help my brain remember. I am no longer skilled at multi-tasking, although I can do complex reasoning and problem solving. I need to slow down and to focus my attention.

My mental and physical endurance are lower. I now need to sleep eight hours a night rather than four to six. At some point in the evening, after a full day, it is as if my mental lights go out, as if I hit a wall. Day is done, and time for bed.

Fatiguing more easily and with a small measure of background pain in my bones and muscles, I see fewer clients than in pre-accident days. I do my best to avoid rushing and stressing myself. I also avoid multi-tasking now, which I used to experience as fun. I still have some complementary/alternative treatments to help my body and brain maintain optimal functioning: massage, acupuncture, chiropractic treatments, plus other types of body/somatic therapies as needed. I am fortunate to live in an area where all this is available, to have the insurance and resources that enable these treatments. However, I am not a trust funder, and financial survival has also been a complicated beast for me, given all the costs of missed work, decreased work, and the myriad of treatments and medical care needed.

My accident affected my physical strength as well as my vision. For instance, I am still an expert skier, but I have to work harder to maintain my equilibrium, have less quick physical flexibility, and have to be more careful in what I choose to do.

Because of my head injury, I also now have a statistically higher risk of getting Alzheimer's than I had before my big accident. My mother had Alzheimer's, and her mother had dementia. I hope that I have my father's cognitive genes, as he lived clear-minded to an old age. I cope by keeping my mind active with work and interests, learning new things, doing math the old fashioned way before I check my work with a calculator; by regular aerobic exercise, healthy eating, good sleep, and times of rest, relaxation, and laughter; by telling myself that I may have my father's cognitive genes; by having my acupuncturist give me "brain points" every time I see her, and by taking recommended vitamins and herbs that support brain health.

As I write, I am struck by the power of tuning into our eyes and hearing. Eyes have been called the windows to the soul. Sound, especially music, has been called the universal language. Hearing is the major sense organ (when available) for people with eye/vision impairment, and vision/use of the eyes is the major sense organ (when available) for people with hearing impairment. Hearing is the last sensation to go in a coma: people who have functional auditory nerves can often hear even if they are apparently unresponsive (like Gerry). In my nursing days, many ICU patients who survived comas and near death experiences afterward thanked me for my support by talking to them while they returned to conscious life. As I reflect on Gerry's blinking to communicate when he was "brain dead," on the fire in my eyes recognized by those who most intimately knew me and were able to help me reclaim my life, and even on Nancy's long, final gazes of love shortly before she died, I want to encourage us all to never forget to look carefully into the eyes of a traumatized person. We need to assess presence through any response (however subtle) such as the capacity to blink or determined scanning of the environment, even through loving gaze in the process of saying goodbye, and to also be careful and positive in what we say in the presence of people who cannot see or are in apparent coma.

I was correct in my self-assessment when going through the discharge process from the Bay Area hospital for inpatient rehabilitation in May 2000: my right eye/cranial nerve damage created more problems than my brain did in my day-to-day life, affecting vision, balance, pain, and appearance. It also required extensive treatments (daily eye exercises; many different Western and Eastern (complementary/alternative), i.e. Integrative Medicine[6] treatments) and three eye surgeries, all of which cost much time and money. My brain functioning allowed me to return to work as well as to manage all my healthcare/healing needs within a few months, and to re-engage in my complex life. But the aberrant nerve regeneration affecting my right eye was the hardest thing for me to accept. Instead of my dogged determination for perfect physical healing, it felt wise to let go, to accept where I was with deep appreciation for all my healers as well as for the regenerative genius of the human body. Eventually this became a conduit for literally and metaphorically shifting my view, for teaching me about the need for and ultimate relief in true acceptance.

It was time to focus on a less intense regime of maintenance treatments, to have more time to get on with my life. I wanted to start writing this book, which had begun forming in my mind while still in the hospital after my accident.

My new understanding of full healing is not necessarily equivalent to the 100% wholeness of a healthy young body. For me, the process of seeking full healing became: doing all I can to help my body, mind, emotions, and soul live as fully as possible given what currently is true in my health and life. This process eventually led to peace in spirit, acceptance of what is, and gratitude for what is possible. It took many years of work for me to arrive at this view of acceptance.

In addition, full healing is not necessarily lack of disease or avoidance of inevitable death. We naturally change and usually physically decline as we age and move toward death. And so it is. Hopefully we get to live long enough to get older over time. Moving to acceptance along the way helped me learn to gently tolerate the inevitable aging process.

"Gratitude as a discipline involves a conscious choice. I can choose to be grateful even when my emotions and feelings are steep and hurt and resentful. It is amazing how many occasions present themselves in which I can choose gratitude instead of complaint."

Henri Nouwen, 1992[1]

Having known Carole since our first year in graduate school, I can attest that she was deeply and sincerely "spiritual" before spiritual was au courant in our profession, defined as a deep sense of belonging, of wholeness, of connectedness, and of openness to the infinite. This ineffable quality pervaded all aspects of her remarkable life even before the accident.

And I have no doubt that what has pulled Carole through has been these strong spiritual sensibilities, in addition to her physical resiliency, a mind that simply won't quit, and the kind of profound bonds with people where she inspired a small tribe utterly devoted to her recovery. I've never seen anything quite like it.

It is then fitting that Carole chooses to make the final chapter of this book on the subject of her gratitude, perhaps an odd theme in the minds of some given what she has lived through. Yet as Nouwen made clear, gratitude is an act of will for what's most challenging in life, as well as for all that's beautiful and lovely. Consequently Nouwen wove this theme into his meditation on the Wounded Healer, and there could be no finer example than Carole.

In closing, those of us who know and love Carole especially appreciate her French heritage—manifest variously in her last name, her extended travels to her family there, her delight with French food and cooking and hospitality, and generally living with a Gallic sparkle in her eye. Therefore it seems fitting to finish with a French proverb for it captures the essence of what Carole has shared with us in this memoir.

"Gratitude is a memory of the heart."[2]

(Reflection by John White,[3] friend and colleague, 2014.)

24

Gratitude

Gratitude promotes health, healing, and a sense of wellbeing. However, gratitude can feel very far away when we are in shock, hurting, struggling, fearful, angry, grieving, in pain physically, emotionally, mentally, interpersonally, socially, existentially, and spiritually.

I hate it when people suggest forgiveness and gratitude prematurely. That feels trite and disingenuous, like a pressure based on belief rather than a natural outflowing from deep inner work.

I am not a phony person, and I would never encourage others to take on phony attitudes or stances. Yet I have learned since my accident that practicing awareness of gratitude—and forgiveness—can foster my genuine experience of them and the opening of my heart.

It was easy to feel a measure of gratitude within the first two months following my accident. I felt gratitude and awe at the mere fact that I was alive after such an accident, for the help from Toby[4] and all those others who joined his helping me in the tree well right after my accident. I felt gratitude for excellent physicians and healers, and I expressed this either in person or on the phone as often as possible. I felt gratitude for family and friends who supported and loved me through the twisted labyrinth of my accident and healing. In time, I came to feel gratitude for my financial need to return to work, which motivated me to actively pursue healing so that I would be well enough to work again. I always feel gratitude for the heartfelt, mentally invigorating, spiritually moving work that I am blessed to do, for the people I work with in my office who risk being open and vulnerable with me, trusting me to be of help.

Other types of gratitude have been much slower in coming. Now years later, I feel gratitude for all I have learned through this tough experience, though I would never have actively wished for or chosen this pilgrimage. My heart and feelings of love are broader, my acceptance and peace in life deeper, anxiety and fear lessened. All this change allows me to rest in more quiet inner stillness. I live more in the now than before my accident, and I enjoy with appreciation every moment of my life in a more poignant way. My work feels even more expansive than before. Also, I am able to experience the joy of sharing what I have learned with you. I hope that sharing my journey is meaningful and helpful to you.

So, in my experience, gratitude[5] came in different time stages, at different levels, with different meanings. Just like acceptance, gratitude needed to come from inner connection with myself, and also with others. It blossomed naturally from within by receiving and giving love, and from spiritual attunement.

I could not even think of gratitude during the initial stages of my accident. I was in fight mode and angry, trying to survive. However, thankfulness for all the help, love, and healing I received was natural to experience when my consciousness began to emerge after halting the use of strong drugs. It took years for me to notice that when I focus more on my experience of gratitude, I feel greater happiness, peace, meaning in life, even joy.

Another way I express gratitude is to mark special anniversary dates by celebrating life with my loved ones. For instance, we celebrate April 16th every year, the anniversary of my big accident. This celebration is a bit different each year, made to order as we need and want each time. As part of celebrating, I thank God for my life, for my actually being alive, and I thank those nearby for their help and sustaining love. Another example is celebrating my mother's life on the anniversary of her birth and her death, either by doing something she would have enjoyed or making a donation in her honor. Doing this helps me appreciate the love, special memories and experiences she gave me. With each anniversary celebration of dear ones, including big life experiences for those still here, I pray for wisdom in how to live more helpfully and compassionately, something I am continually learning.

It is my hope that by sharing some of the relevant stories of my accident, some of the miracles that followed, some of what I learned, that you will be able to tune in more to yourself and to your loved ones. I hope that you will have a deeper sense of when and how to reach out for help—in any way you need it. I also hope that you will be able to tune in more to the amazing synchronicities and gifts in your own life. May my stories broaden and deepen your own resonance with your stories.

Namaste,
Carole Petiet

(Feel welcome to contact me via my website: www.carolepetietphd.com.)

Appendix: Alternative/ Complementary Adjunctive Treatments To Heal My Eye And Vision

Always ask your medical doctor if these are safe for you, before trying.
Note: all homeopathic pills/pellets should be placed with no touching by fingers or hands; use top of dispenser to get right number to the area under your tongue (sublingual).

A) Alternative medicines to prepare before and heal after eye surgery:

Begin the following homeopathic and enzyme pills and ointments/creams a week before eye surgery and continue for a week past evidence of bruising after eye surgery:

1. Bromelain 500mg 1-2 tablets daily with food (natural enzyme from pineapple known to reduce inflammation).
2. Traumeel/Traumed tablet 1 four times a day sublingual (homeopathic).
3. Traumeel/Traumed or Arnica homeopathic cream/gel two to three times a day on intact skin.
4. Arnica Montana 200 five homeopathic pellets sublingual three times a day.

B) Adjunctive treatments that helped heal cranial nerves that control eye and lid muscles:

1. CranioSacral therapy.
2. Acupuncture (some with electrical stimulation).
3. Eye exercises (see Chapter 11 plus Notes and Resources for details).
4. Somatic Experiencing® therapy.
5. Massage therapy, including focused work with occiput.
6. Physical therapy as needed.
7. General aerobic exercise, increasing up to an hour five times a week.
8. Healthy eating, relaxation/rest/sleep, stress reduction.
9. Therapeutic eye massage, neuromuscular massage with eye focus, Filipino and other spiritual healing; these methods worked less well for the healing of my eye, yet I was doing 1 – 8 above.

Notes and Resources

Throughout the book I have given the full names of excellent professionals who were helpful to me. In these Notes I provide their titles and locations, in case you want to contact them—as well as additional resources related to the content of each chapter. Other professionals that I experienced as unhelpful or worse are referred to in this book with their names omitted. I have provided contact information for friends described in this book who are still working and have professional skills, in case you want to contact them. Other friends are included in the Acknowledgements.

There is valuable information—in these Notes and Resources—about a number of topics related to chapters in this book as shown in my narrative, including: Integrative Medicine for healing, brain plasticity, healing of eyes, treatment of trauma, Somatic Experiencing®, somatic therapy, ski safety, humor, gratitude, and helping children after a parent has trauma.

Preface

1 Nicole Petiet is my daughter: same Note as for Chapter 17.

2 Margaret Allen, PhD, friend and colleague, was a psychologist in Berkeley, CA. She is now deceased.

Foreword

1 Professor Ayala Malach Pines, PhD, 1945-2012. Ayala received her PhD at Boston University. Internationally renowned in social, organizational,

and clinical psychology, Ayala was a pioneer in the study of burnout and love. She published 10 books plus many book chapters and research papers throughout her professional career. Ayala's last professorship was as Dean of the Faculty of Management at Ben-Gurion University in Israel. She was a beloved teacher, author, psychotherapist, colleague, family member, and friend—truly irreplaceable.

Chapter 1: Family Fun Race: The Day I Died

1 Toby Rowland-Jones, former volunteer firefighter and rescue responder, is grateful to have been at the right place and the right time. He currently lives in Monterey, CA, leads the Big Sur Food and Wine Festival, and is also sommelier at Grasing's of Carmel. Toby, who saved my life, can be reached via email: toby@survision.net.

2 Trauma Blue is called to provide the most concentrated and sophisticated level of trauma care for a patient.

3 Steven R. Kennedy, MD, Emergency Physician, Renown Regional Medical Center, 1155 Mill St., Reno, NV 89502; 775-982-4100.

4 Jay K. Morgan, MD, FAANS, Neurosurgeon; Sierra Neurosurgery Group, 5590 Kietzke Lane, Reno, NV 89511; 775-323-2080; now Chief of Neurosurgery at Renown Regional Medical Center, Reno, NV.

Chapter 2: Trauma Care, Acute Care

1 Jay Morgan, MD: same Note as for Chapter 1.

2 Margaret Allen, PhD: same Note as for Preface.

3 Jim Pettit, PhD, is one of my brothers, the second of four children in our original family. He is a retired fireman and EMT-I, a working teacher and a Marriage and Family Therapist in the Dallas, TX area; 214-538-2788.

4 Dave Pettit is my youngest brother. He lives near Portland, OR, does private consultation with computer networking, Internet technology, and is a writer; 503-684-4030.

5 Marilee Stark, PhD, is an educator, writer, and has a psychotherapy practice in Lafayette, CA, and a coaching practice in Berkeley, CA; 510-343-9216.

Chapter 3: Into Rehab

1 Jill Bolte Taylor, PhD, *My Stroke of Insight: A Brain Scientist's Personal Journey* (New York: Plume, Penguin, 2009), 80.

Taylor's book is a brilliant memoir of her cerebral vascular accident (stroke) when 37 years old, as a Harvard-trained brain scientist. She tells her personal journey after unexpected brain trauma, and she also includes a uniquely clear and understandable description of brain functioning, which she calls "simple science," 9-35.

Taylor's memoir poignantly describes what she needed most in her brain injured state, including:

"I desperately needed people to treat me as though I would recover completely." 116

"I needed the people around me to believe in the plasticity of my brain and its ability to grow, learn, and recover." 117

"For a successful recovery, it was important that we focus on my ability, not my disability." 123

"I needed people to come close and not be afraid of me." 125

Taylor's words touched me deeply when I read them nine years after my accident. I strongly recommend her book for anyone going through a brain trauma.

2 Jay Morgan, MD: same Note as for Chapter 1.

Chapter 4: Out of the Cage: Overcoming Problems in the Rehab Unit

1 Kathryn Ridall, PhD, friend and colleague, helped me name and understand the "brain injury grid" that I was experiencing and upset about after my accident. Kathryn is currently in Ventura, CA, still practicing psychotherapy as well as writing poetry. She can be reached at: 143 Figeuroa St., Ventura, CA 93001; 541-968-4297; www.kathryn-ridall.com.

2 T.M. Fields, "Massage Therapy Effects," *American Psychologist* 53, no. 12 (1998): 1270-1281. Research benefits of massage therapy were reviewed and reported, including multiple trials of: enhancing growth, pain reduction, and attentiveness; reducing neuromuscular problems; alleviating stress, depression, and anxiety; helping decrease eating disorders, cortisol levels, cardiovascular symptoms of stress, chronic fatigue, diabetes, asthma, and immune disorders; and increasing a sense of physical well-being while

coping with cancer. There have been many newer research articles on the health benefits of massage therapy.

3 Joan Provencher, trained in therapeutic massage, jin shin jyutsu, and kairos, lives in Berkeley, CA; contact: 510-525-2750.

4 Paul Watzlawick, *The Situation Is Hopeless, But Not Serious (The Pursuit of Unhappiness)* (New York: W.W. Norton & Company, 1993).

Chapter 5: Oh, My Head ...

1 Brenda D. Townes, PhD, neuropsychologist, is now retired and Professor Emeritus, Department of Psychiatry and Behavioral Sciences, University of Washington School of Medicine: btownes@u.washington.edu. As a professor, Brenda has published numerous articles on neuropsychological assessment and behavior.

I first met Brenda Townes in 1985 when she helped me devise the research protocol for studying the effects of high altitude mountaineering on women, data gathered while I was a participant in the first all women's climbing expedition in the Chinese Himalaya in 1986. This was subsequently published as:

Petiet, Townes, Brooks, & Kramer, "Neurobehavioral and Psychosocial Functioning of Women Exposed to High Altitude in Mountaineering," *Perceptual and Motor Skills* 67, (1988): 443-452.

2 Margaret Allen, PhD: same as Note for Preface.

3 See the following Somatic Experiencing® therapy book that is specifically focused on overcoming physical pain:

Peter A. Levine and Maggie Phillips, *Freedom from Pain: Discover Your Body's Power to Overcome Physical Pain* (Boulder, CO: Sounds True, 2012). This is available in CD, paperback that includes a CD, and electronic forms.

Chapter 6: Post-Narcotic Rapid Recovery

1 Kenneth H. Cooper, MD, MPH, *Aerobics* (New York: Bantam, 1968). Dr. Cooper, "The Father of Aerobics," established the Cooper Institute in 1970 and left the U.S. Air Force where he had been a flight surgeon and director of the Aerospace Medical Laboratory. See: www.cooperinstitute.org; 800-635-7050. Also see: www.cooperaerobics.com; 866-906-2667. Dr. Cooper has written 18 books since *Aerobics* and is a leading pioneer of

Preventive Medicine. Dr. Cooper, born in 1931, is still aerobically active and working in the clinic at the Cooper Aerobics Center (January 2016).

2 Joan Provencher: same as Note for Chapter 4. Joan is also a mountain climber, and I first met her on the all women's climbing expedition in the Chinese Himalaya (Mt. Kongur) in 1986.

3 Rachel Naomi Remen, MD, *Kitchen Table Wisdom: Stories That Heal* (New York: Penguin, 2006), 114 & 118. (See also further Note for Chapter 13: about Dr. Remen's pioneering work in Integrative Medicine.)

Chapter 7: Breaking Free: Negotiating My Way Beyond the Box

1 Doctors who were at the hospital for inpatient rehabilitation are not named for protection of their identity and for good karma on my part; they know who they are.

Chapter 8: Inner Landscape

1 Phillip L. Berman, *The Journey Home: What Near-Death Experiences and Mysticism Teach Us About the Gift of Life* (New York: Pocket Books, Simon & Schuster, 1996).

Phillip Berman is a Harvard theologian who described universal truths culled from personal experience and hundreds of interviews of persons who had a near death experience (NDE). In summary, a NDE teaches us about the gift of life and provides lessons that transform feelings leading to experiencing less fear and more appreciation of life, self-love, compassion, and meaning.

2 Paul Kalamithi and Abraham Verghese (Foreword), *When Breath Becomes Air* (New York: Penguin Random House, 2016). This powerful memoir of dying and the joy of living, was written by a neurosurgeon as he was dying and after his death was completed by his physician wife.

3 Peter A. Levine, *In An Unspoken Voice: How the Body Releases Trauma and Restores Goodness* (Berkeley, CA: North Atlantic Books, 2010). (See further Notes for Chapter 16).

4 The impact of narcotics on my memory and brain functioning caused me to try other pain management strategies as soon as I could. These are listed in Chapter 5.

5 My body's response to trauma initially caused me to seek body therapies including: massage therapy, acupuncture, lymphatic massage, and craniosacral therapy. Eventually I sought Somatic Experiencing® therapy and studied this powerful form of treating residual responses in the body after experiences of trauma. See www.traumahealing.org for information about the Somatic Experiencing Trauma Institute™, including written information, videos, and referral to trained practitioners (a rapidly growing network around the world). See also the United States Association for Body Psychotherapy at: www.usabp.org, and the International Body Psychotherapy Journal for a variety of treatment approaches for trauma via focus on the body.

Peter Levine, who developed Somatic Experiencing®, received the Lifetime Achievement Award from the United States Association for Body Psychotherapy in 2010.

Chapter 9: One Step at a Time: Coping with Many Mini-Traumas

1 Dave Pettit: same Note as for Chapter 2, with his wife Kelley.
2 Helen Hempel, JD, now moved to California: www.hempellaw.com; Helen B Hempel, CELA*, Attorney at Law, 306 Capitol Street, Salinas, CA 93901; 831-754-1431; email at: Helen@hempellaw.com. *Certified as an Elder Law Attorney by the National Elder Law Foundation.
3 Margaret Allen, PhD: same Note as for Preface.

Chapter 10: Beyond Limitations, Broken Mirrors

1 Kathryn Ridall, PhD, friend and colleague, helped me name and understand the "broken mirrors" that I was experiencing and upset about after my accident; see same contact information as in Note for Chapter 4.
2 Richard L. Litwin, MD, is now at 2999 Regent St. #425, Berkeley, CA 94705; 510-548-6630; see www.bomg.org.
3 Ram Dass, *Still Here: Embracing Aging, Changing, and Dying* (New York: Riverhead Books of Penguin Putnam, 2000); see www.ramdass.org.
4 Body therapies and psychotherapies; see same Notes as for Chapters 8 and 16.

Chapter 11: Shifting My View

1 Jean Mayer owns and operates the Hotel St. Bernard in Taos Ski Valley, New Mexico. He is also the technical director of the ski school there. More about Jean in Chapter 20.

2 Martyn ___, MD, I deeply regret that I only have the spelling of your first name, from my personal journal, when I met you at the St. B in Taos, February-March 2001. I did every amount of research possible to retrieve your last name and to locate you again, to properly thank you for your astute and generous help in getting me to see Dr. Stuart Seiff, who subsequently did two excellent surgeries on my right eye, in 2001 and 2005. My computer died in 2001, and I changed my email address. I hope you are very well. Please contact me if you ever read this book.

3 Richard L. Litwin, MD: same Note as for Chapter 10.

4 See further Integrative Medicine Notes for Chapters 13 and 19.

5 UCSF is the University of California School of Medicine in San Francisco.

6 Richard K. Imes, MD, California Pacific Medical Center, 2340 Clay St., San Francisco, CA 94115; 415-600-3901.

7 Rachel N. Remen, MD: same Note as for Chapter 6, (2006), 235. See also Note for Chapter 13.

8 Carole Anne Petiet, "Grief in Divorcees and Widows: Similarities, Differences, and Treatment Implications" (PhD dissertation, CSPP-Berkeley, CA, 1982). The article: "Hope: The Strongest Predictor" was extracted from this dissertation and presented at the annual American Psychological Association meeting in L.A., CA (1983). Subsequently, I was interviewed about that paper, and an article was published on the front page of *USA Today* (for 2/14/1985).

9 Lynn K. Segura, LAc, 2615 Ashby Ave., Berkeley, CA 94705; 510-843-8889; www.lynnsegura.com. Lynn Segura has a kind, calm presence and is tuned into Holistic Medicine.

10 Greg Schelkun, 700 E St., San Rafael, CA 94901; 415-459-0680.

11 CranioSacral Therapy (CST) is a gentle type of hands-on work with bones in the head and surrounding the nervous system in the spinal cord to the sacrum, also working with subtle movements of the cerebral spinal fluid, "the rhythm of life." CST was pioneered and developed by osteopathic physician John E. Upledger; see www.upledger.com.

12 Cathy Adachi is a registered physical therapist (RPT) in private practice. She is multiply skilled in hands-on work, was trained in Eutony, Feldenkrais, and various manual therapies including CranioSacral Therapy, Visceral

Manipulation, Mechanical Link, and Lymphatic Drainage Therapy. Cathy returned to the East Bay, CA in 2011: 510-374-6289.

13 Katrina Auer, CST, is presumably still in North Carolina, but I have been unable to locate her.

14 Stuart R. Seiff, MD, FACS, is in practice at: 2100 Webster St. #214, San Francisco, CA 94115; 415-923-3007; www.pacificeye.com. Dr. Seiff retired as Director of Ophthalmic Plastic and Reconstructive Surgery at UCSF Medical School and is now Emeritus Professor of Ophthalmology at UCSF.

15 Meir Schneider, PhD, School for Self-Healing, 2218 48th Ave., San Francisco, CA 94116; 415-665-9574, www.self-healing.org, is the author of a number of books and CDs that can be found on his website, including *Self-Healing: My Life and Vision* (Arkana, 1988). See also:

Meir Schneider, *Vision for Life: Ten Steps to Natural Eyesight Improvement* (Berkeley, CA: North Atlantic Books, 2012).

I met Jane Battenberg, MA, DCH, in a hot tub in Mammoth, California, when I was there in the early 2000s with our Tahoe women's ski group (aka Betties on Boards) for our annual trip. Jane joined our group for a number of years. Jane, who studied with Meir Schneider among others, published with her sister an excellent eye exercise book that can be found on www.Amazon.com:

Dr. Jane Rigney Battenberg and Martha M. Rigney, *Eye Yoga – How You See is How You Think* (Minneapolis, MN: Langdon Street Press, 2010).

16 Classic anxiety and stress symptoms that I experienced while challenging my body to relearn athletic skills and to learn new eye exercises included: rapid heart rate, hyperventilation, feeling dizzy, fatigue, muscle twitching around my eyes, neck and shoulder tightness, brief disorientation, and feeling of being overwhelmed and distracted. These stress symptoms were coped with and decreased over time by deep breathing, orienting myself in time and space, talking kindly to myself like a best friend or loving mother would ("positive self-talk," a cognitive behavioral technique), and by practice, practice, practice.

17 Creig S. Hoyt, MD, MA, Emeritus Professor and Chair, Ophthalmology Department, UCSF Medical School.

18 Douglas R. Fredrick, M.D. is now at the Department of Ophthalmology, Stanford University, Palo Alto, CA; 650-723-6995. When responding to my fact checking, he wrote: "Thank you for writing this memoir – it demonstrates the power of resilience and value of determination and perseverance. … I think all that you say is factual and accurate. … Thanks for writing this book – it will help others."

19 Kathy L. Kain, MA, SEP lives in the Bay Area, CA, and teaches in Europe, Australia, Canada, and throughout the U. S. She has practiced and taught bodywork and trauma recovery skills for over 34 years. Her trainings cover various focus areas including: trauma recovery, somatic touch, self-regulation skills, and resilience. These focus areas ultimately weave together forming a unified somatic approach to touch, awareness, and relationship. Kathy is one of the Senior Faculty in the Somatic Experiencing Trauma Institute™ training program and can be seen on the SETI website www.traumahealing.org, developed Touch Skills Training for Trauma Therapists, is an adjunct faculty member of Sonoma State University, and offers her own workshops via her Somatic Practice programs; see www.somaticpractice.net. (She may also be reached at P.O. Box 1447, Millbrae, CA 94030.)

Her excellent book is available at www.Amazon.com: Kathy L. Kain with Jim Berns, *Ortho-Bionomy: A Practical Manual* (Berkeley, CA: North Atlantic Books, 1997).

Chapter 12: Humor Helps, Too

1 Susan Phillips, PhD, is a friend and colleague who joined our women's spiritual group in the early 1990s. Susan is multi-talented professionally: a sociologist and social psychologist, spiritual director, Executive Director of New College in Berkeley, and international teacher, speaker, and retreat leader. Susan is also an author. Her books and contact information are reached via: www.susansphillips.com. Susan's books that are relevant to my book include:

Susan S. Phillips, *The Cultivated Life: From Ceaseless Striving to Receiving Joy* (Downers Grove, IL: InterVarsity Press, 2015).

Susan S. Phillips, *Candlelight: Illuminating the Art of Spiritual Direction* (Harrisburg, PA – New York: Moorehouse Publishing, 2008).

Susan S. Phillips and Patricia Benner, eds., *The Crisis of Care: Affirming and Restoring Caring Practices in the Helping Professions* (Washington, DC: Georgetown University Press, 1994).

2 Priya Yerasi, MD, Internal Medicine doctor, decided after having young children to leave the Bay Area where she was in private practice in Oakland and moved to work at Kaiser in Southern CA and to be closer to extended family. She is at Kaiser Permanente Orange County - Anaheim Medical Center, 3440 E. La Palma Ave. Anaheim, CA 92806; 714-644-2000.

3 Lynn Segura, LAc: same Note as for Chapter 11.

4 I have come to understand the value of humor by watching friends and clients use it to cope with chronic and terminal illnesses. Much has been written on the health and coping benefits of humor and laughter (which is a physiological response).

See: www.humormatters.com by Steven M. Sultanoff, PhD.

In fact, humor produces psychological and physiological effects on the body that are similar to the health benefits of aerobic exercise. See:

R.A. Berk, "The Active Ingredients in Humor: Psychological Benefits and Risks for Older Adults," *Educational Gerontology* 27, no. 3-4 (2001): 323-339.

Physiologically, laughter results in: decreased serum cortisol (stress response hormone), increased immunoglobulin A (increasing the body's immune response), increased pain tolerance; it directly changes distressing emotions, such as depression, anger, and anxiety, so it may decrease the risk of heart and other diseases. For example, see:

W. Christie and C. Moore, "The Impact of Humor on Patients with Cancer," *Clinical Journal of Oncology Nursing* 9, no. 2/April (2005): 211-218.

Chapter 13: Healers and the Whole Person

1 Priya Yerasi, MD: same Note as for Chapter 12.

2 Irene Pech, MD, PhD, was in private practice in Oakland, CA; unable to currently locate her in a neurology practice.

3 Neurontin: see description of this medicine in Chapter 5.

4 Rehab Without Walls: see www.rehabwithoutwalls.com. The group I worked with is out of: Rehab Without Walls, Northern CA/Bay Area, 2155 S. Bascom Ave., Suite 103, Campbell, CA 95008; 408-559-9020 or 866-734-2296. Rehab Without Walls currently has providers in areas in 12 states (2015).

5 George Pugh, MD, orthopedist, had offices in Oakland and Orinda. He recently retired.

6 Ben Gilbert, PT, was at Berkeley Physical Therapy, 2041 Bancroft Way #301, Berkeley, CA 94704; 510-549-2225.

7 Scott R. Phillips, DC, now has his office at 2006 Dwight Way #108, Berkeley, CA 94704; 510-644-4425; see: www.drscottphillips.com. I also saw:

8 David W. Doan, DC, who works in the same office as Dr. Scott Phillips above; also at 510-644-4425. Both chiropractors are kind, gentle, and

helpful. I saw them off and on for just over three years, as my broken cervical spine healed.

9 In 2006 I fell in a situation related to visual depth perception difficulties in poor lighting as a result of my big ski accident. I needed a different kind of chiropractor to help my displaced pelvis and hip, and I had the good fortune of being referred to a multimodal chiropractor after a month of incorrect diagnoses by a number of doctors while my pain and immobility increased. This new to me chiropractor was able to diagnose me properly and skillfully help me get realigned, so my legs once again became the same length and I could walk again without pain. This is an example of learning to say "Next," as described by my teenage client in Chapter 13, when I needed to change providers to helpfully treat a new healthcare problem. One skill set was needed closer to my big ski accident, and a different skill set was needed six years later. I saw:

David K. Chan, DC, who was practicing in San Francisco and now has his office in Mountain View: 1580 W. El Camino Real, Suite 4, Mountain View, CA 94040; 650-969-1212. His office can be reached for communication via email: drchanchiropractor@gmail.com. Dr. Chan is also kind, gentle, and helpful.

Since receiving this help from Dr. Chan and thereby understanding the importance of proper body alignment for pain free and maximal physical functioning—physical therapists and good chiropractors are skilled at helping alignment with hands-on techniques, as are some body therapists—I have continued to see Dr. Chan monthly, to help my body function optimally. Over the years, after assessing my alignment at the beginning of each session, he has used: electrical stimulation along with steamed heat packs, deep massage with specialized lotions, manual manipulations (he has several different approaches for each problem, and uses the best one for each whole-body situation), traction, laser, and ultra sound.

10 Integrative Medicine is becoming more mainstream in the U.S., thanks to six pioneers who are teachers, researchers, authors and have taught and inspired many other practitioners:

Larry Dossey, MD, is best known as an advocate for the role of the mind and spirit in health. Learn more about his work and books via: www.larrydosseymd.com.

James Gordon, MD, a psychiatrist, is one of the first people to develop the practical foundation of mind-body medicine. Under the auspices of NIMH, he developed the first major text in the field, and he is the Founder and Director of The Center for Mind-Body Medicine. Learn more about his work and books via: www.jamesgordonmd.com.

Jon Kabat-Zinn, PhD, is best known for bringing mindfulness into the mainstream of medicine and society. He does not have a personal professional website, but his work and books can be seen by googling his name.

Dean Ornish, MD, is best known for his groundbreaking work with cardiovascular disease, demonstrating through research that integrative medicine interventions may reverse the progression of coronary heart disease without the use of drugs or surgery. Learn more about his work and books via: www.deanornish.com.

Rachel Naomi Remen, MD, is one of the first pioneers in the mind-body holistic health movement, including the role of the spirit in health and recovery from illness. Together with Michael Lerner, she founded the Cancer Help Program at Commonweal, in Bolinas, CA. She designed in 1991 a medical student curriculum called "The Healer's Art," used in 70+ medical schools in the U.S. and internationally. Learn more about her work and books via: www.rachelremen.com.

Andrew Weil, MD, is internationally recognized as an expert on integrative medicine, medicinal plants and mind-body interactions. He is the founder, director, and a professor of the Arizona Center for Integrative Medicine at the University of Arizona. Learn more about his work and books via: www.drweil.com.

Chapter 14: Unexpected Benefits

See more about Integrative Medicine in: Notes for Chapter 13.

1 Lynn Segura, LAc: same as Note for Chapter 11.

2 Jin Shin Jyutsu is an ancient oriental Art of releasing tensions and harmonizing life energy within the body.

3 Cathy Adachi, RPT: same Note as for Chapter 11.

Chapter 15: Return to Work: Challenges and Gifts

1 Canadian Mountain Holidays (CMH) is the heli-ski company that operates the Monashees Lodge. See Chapter 20 and Note for Chapter 20 for more information about CMH.

2 Carrie D. Thaler, PhD, is a licensed psychologist in private practice in Albany, CA. She specializes in rehabilitation neuropsychology and

psychoanalytic psychotherapy and maintains a general psychotherapy practice. Call at: 510-565-7444; see: www.carriedthalerphd.com.

I saw Carrie Thaler via Rehab Without Walls: same as Note for Chapter 13.

3 Dan Taube, JD, PhD (attorney and psychologist), can be reached at One Beach Street, Suite 100, San Francisco, CA 94133; 415-336-8060; or via email: dtaube@alliant.edu and 415-955-2125.

4 Much has recently been written on brain plasticity, brain retraining, and nerve regeneration. Excellent resources include:

Norman Doidge, MD, *The Brain That Changes Itself: Stories of Personal Triumph from the Frontiers of Brain Science* (New York: Penguin Group, 2007). Dr. Doidge is a Canadian-born psychiatrist and psychoanalyst; he is on Facebook.com.

Norman Doidge, MD, *The Brain's Way of Healing: Remarkable Discoveries and Recoveries from the Frontiers of Neuroplasticity* (New York: Viking, Penguin Group, 2015).

Michael Merzenich, PhD, *Soft-Wired: How the New Science of Brain Plasticity Can Change Your Life* (San Francisco: Parnassus Pub, 2nd Edition, 2013). Dr. Merzenich is Professor Emeritus at UCSF and the creator of Brain HQ brain training from Posit Science. "Often called the father of brain plasticity, he is one of the scientists responsible for our current understanding of brain change across the lifespan…." (from back page of his book).

Jill Bolte Taylor, PhD; see Note for Chapter 3. Her memoir also teaches about brain plasticity.

David Roland, *How I Rescued My Brain: A Psychologist's Remarkable Recovery from Stroke and Trauma* (London: Scribe Pubs, 2014). He is on Facebook.com.

Annie Hopper, *Wired for Healing – Remapping the Brain to Recover from Chronic and Mysterious Illnesses* (2014); can be ordered on www.amazon.com. She is the founder of the Dynamic Neural Retraining System (DNRS), which has received five-star reviews.

Daniel G. Amen, MD, *Making A Good Brain Great* (New York: Three Rivers Press, 2005).

Daniel G. Amen, MD, *Healing the Hardware of the Soul: Enhance Your Brain to Improve your Work, Love, and Spiritual Life* (New York, Free Press, 2002).

Daniel G. Amen, MD, *Change your Brain, Change Your Life* (New York: Three Rivers Press, 1998).

Many books about brain training can be seen on www.amazon.com

under "brain plasticity books," and many of these are in Kindle editions only. Only one of the above books, Amen (1998) was written before my accident (2000), and it was focused mostly on the brain and psychiatric disorders.

While still in the hospital for inpatient rehabilitation, I was referred to a book focused on the brain not working well enough to return to prior professional work. This book has been suggested to many patients in rehabilitation programs, for the purpose of understanding, accepting, and recovering as well as possible from the impact of Traumatic Brain Injury (TBI):

Claudia L. Osborn, *Over My Head: A Doctor's Own Story of Head Injury from the Inside Looking Out* (Kansas City: Andrews McMeel Pub, 1998).

I fortunately was able to return to my professional work, even before all the current understandings, writings, and approaches that focus on working with brain plasticity and the possibility of more complete recovery. I believe my fortunate recovery was due to good luck, a lifetime of healthy practices, and then learning how to expand my Integrative Medicine practices to include the somatic therapy work of healing from my inside out (see also Chapters 13 & 16, including their Notes and Resources).

Chapter 16: Healing From Inside Out

1 Esalen is: Esalen Institute – Big Sur, CA, on Highway 1. See: www.esalen.org or call 831-667-3000.

2 Marcia Black, PhD, is a friend and colleague who has a private practice in San Francisco and in Oakland, CA; call 415-554-3635. Marcia can be found on: www.linkedin.com and also Marcia Black Practitioner Details - SE Practitioner Directory.

3 Peter Levine, PhD, is the founder of Somatic Experiencing®, a body-awareness approach to trauma. (See also Notes for Chapter 8.) He developed SETI: Somatic Experiencing Trauma Institute™. For much information on the SE™ model, including a list of trained practitioners across the U.S. and internationally, see details on www.traumahealing.org.

Please note: Somatic Experiencing®, SE™, SETI™ and Somatic Experiencing Trauma Institute™ are trademarks owned by Peter A. Levine, PhD, or SE Trauma Institute, and may not be used or applied without written consent.

4 Provided here are the major books on healing via SE™ (two with CDs):

Peter A. Levine, *Waking the Tiger: Healing Trauma* (Berkeley, CA: North Atlantic Books, 1997).

Diane Poole Heller and Laurence Heller, *Crash Course: A Self-Healing Guide to Auto Accident Trauma and Recovery* (Berkeley, CA: North Atlantic Books, 2001).

Peter A. Levine, *Healing Trauma: A Pioneering Program for Restoring the Wisdom of Your Body* (Boulder, CO: Sounds True, 2005). This includes a paperback book and a CD with 12 guided SE exercises.

Peter A. Levine and Maggie Kline, *Trauma Through A Child's Eyes: Awakening the Ordinary Miracle of Healing* (Berkeley, CA: North Atlantic Books, 2007).

Peter A. Levine and Maggie Kline, *Trauma-Proofing Your Kids: A Parents' Guide for Instilling Confidence, Joy and Resilience* (Berkeley, CA: North Atlantic Books, 2008).

Peter A. Levine, *In An Unspoken Voice: How the Body Releases Trauma and Restores Goodness* (Berkeley, CA: North Atlantic Books, 2010).

Peter A. Levine and Maggie Phillips, *Freedom from Pain…*(2012): same Note as for Chapter 5. This paperback book includes a CD.

Chapter 17: Trauma from Trauma: Helping My Daughter

1 Nicole's "grandmother" is Lois Inman Engle: my beloved friend who later became Nicole's pre-school teacher (now retired). Lois currently is a jewelry and assemblage artist; see her work by googling Lois Inman Engle and then clicking on Artemis Designs or on her Facebook link. (Sadly, Nicole's biological grandparents are no longer alive.)

2 Nicole Petiet can be contacted through me (510-843-6760 or www.carolepetietphd.com).

3 Mirror neurons were first identified by a neuroscience research team while studying monkeys in the 1980s: Giacomo Rizzolotti and Vittorio Gallese at the University of Parma, Italy. In 1996 they dubbed their discovery "mirror neurons." Both of these men can easily be found via Google, including their numerous research articles and also interesting YouTube explanations. The clearest concise article on the Internet about their work, along with Marco Iacoboni who is now a professor at UCLA, can be found at www.scholarpedia.org/article/Mirror_neurons (January 2016); scholarpedia is a peer reviewed open access encyclopedia.

More recent books published about trauma that include understanding of mirror neurons, are:

Allan N. Schore, *Affect Regulation and Repair of the Self* (New York: Norton & Co., 2003).

Daniel J. Siegel and Marion Solomon, eds., *Healing Trauma: Attachment, Mind, Body and Brain, Norton Series on Interpersonal Neurobiology* (New York: Norton & Co., 2003).

Daniel Siegel, MD and Mary Hartzell, MEd, *Parenting From the Inside Out* (New York: Tarcher/Penguin, 2004).

Daniel J. Siegel, *Mindsight: The New Science of Personal Transformation* (New York: Bantom Books, Random House, Inc., 2010).

Daniel J. Siegel, MD, and Tina Payne Bryson, PhD, *The Whole-Brain Child: 12 Revolutionary Strategies to Nurture Your Child's Developing Mind* (New York: Random House, 2011).

Daniel J. Siegel, MD, *The Developing Mind, 2nd Ed: How Relationships and the Brain Interact to Shape Who We Are* (New York: Guilford Publications, Inc., 2012).

Bessel van der Kolk, MD, *The Body Keeps the Score: Brain, Mind, and Body in the Healing of Trauma* (New York: Viking Penguin, 2014).

4 SE™: same Note as for Chapter 16.

5 Mima Baird, PhD, is a friend and psychologist, now retired.

6 Joan Lovett, MD, is the behavioral pediatrician who saw Nicole: 919 The Alameda, Berkeley, CA 94707; 510-524-0488. She wrote:

Joan Lovett, MD, *Small Wonders: Healing Childhood Trauma With EMDR* (New York: The Free Press, Simon & Schuster, Inc., 1999).

7 Francine Shapiro, PhD, who discovered and developed EMDR, has written books for professionals and the general public. See:

Francine Shapiro, PhD, *Eye Movement Desensitization and Reprocessing (EMDR): Basic Principle, Protocols, and Procedures, 2nd Ed.,* (New York: The Guilford Press, 2001).

Francine Shapiro, PhD, Getting Past Your Past: Take Control of Your Life with Self-Help Techniques from EMDR Therapy (New York: Rodale Inc., 2012).

Also see information about EMDR via: www.EMDR.org or www.EMDR.com.

8 Marcia Black, PhD: same Note as for Chapter 16.

9 Ariel Giarretto, LMFT, is a faculty member with the Somatic Experiencing Trauma Institute™ and can be seen on the SETI website: www.traumahealing.org.

10 Julia Morgan School for Girls (JMSG)—see www.juliamorganschool.org, where Nicole attended 7th and 8th grades, was founded after two important books were written that inspired parents, educators, and community members in the East Bay, Northern CA, to come together to envision and create an all-girls' middle school that opened in 1996. These books are:

11 Mary Pipher, PhD, *Reviving Ophelia: Saving the Selves of Adolescent Girls* (New York: Riverhead, Penguin Group, 1994).

12 Peggy Orenstein, *Schoolgirls: Young Women, Self-Esteem, and the Confidence Gap* (New York: Anchor Books, Random House, Inc., 1996).

13 Patch Adams, MD, founded The Gesundheit! Institute in 1971. He can be found at: www.patchadams.org.

14 Camp Winnarainbow is a Circus and Performing Arts Camp in the foothills of Mendocino County near Laytonville in Northern CA. It was founded by Wavy Gravy, and can be found via: www.campwinnarainbow.org.

15 PTSD is Post Traumatic Stress Disorder: see Chapters 20 and 21.

16 April Wise, MFT, was our family therapist. April earned a PsyD in 2015. She can be reached by phone or via her website: 925-253-0740 or www.aprilwisemft.com.

17 Julia Gombos, MFCC, SEP, has private practices in Kentfield (Marin County) and Sebastopol (Sonoma County). Since seeing Nicole, Julia has added the knowledge and skills of the Diamond Approach and Authentic Movement to her multifaceted and deep practice. She can be reached by phone or email: 415-250-9856 or juliagombos@gmail.com.

18 Further major books that discuss the healing of trauma (beyond those already listed in the Chapter 16 Notes) are listed here, and all books can be found on www.amazon.com:

Stephen W. Porges, *The Polyvegal Theory: Neurophysiological Foundations of Emotions, Attachment, Communication, and Self-Regulation* (New York: Norton & Co., 2011).

Susan Pease Banitt, LCSW, *The Trauma Tool Kit: Healing PTSD from the Inside Out* (Wheaton, Ill: Quest Books, 2012).

Linda A. Curran, LPC, *Trauma Competency: A Clinician's Guide* (Eau Claire, WI: PESI, 2010).

Linda A. Curran, LPC, *101 Trauma-Informed Interventions: Activities, Exercises and Assignments to Move the Client and Therapy Forward* (Eau Claire, WI: Premier Pub, CMI Educ. Inst., 2013). This book lists tools and techniques drawn from the most effective trauma modalities.

A classic book in the field of trauma is:

Judith Herman, MD, *Trauma and Recovery: The aftermath of violence—from domestic abuse to political terror* (New York: Basic Books, 1992, 1997).

A book written about the transformational potential of trauma and how it can be used for the mind's development is:

Mark Epstein, MD, *The Trauma of Everyday Life* (New York: Penguin Group, 2013).

Chapter 18: Lifted by Love

1 Mima Baird, PhD: same Note as for Chapter 17.

2 *Holy Bible: King James Version* (New York: The World Publishing Co., 1962).

3 *Good News Bible: Today's English Version* (New York: The American Bible Society, 1966).

4 Nicole Petiet, my daughter: same Note as for Chapter 17. See more of her story in prologue to Chapter 17 and in Chapter 17.

5 Joan Provencher: same Note as for Chapter 4.

6 Dana McMullen, MA, LPCC, LMFT, is a friend and a Marriage and Family Therapist with a practice in Albany, CA; 510-466-1217. See photo and write up by googling Dana McMullen, MFT, Albany, CA, and then click the Psychology Today web link.

7 Margaret Allen, PhD: same Note as for Preface.

8 Rachel Naomi Remen, MD: same Note as for Chapter 6 (2006), 140.

9 Ram Dass: same Note as for Chapter 10.

10 John Lennon and Paul McCartney, *All You Need Is Love* (United Kingdom: BBC, 1967).

Chapter 19: Navigating Institutional Mazes

1 Ioannidis JPA, "Why Most Published Research Findings Are False," PLoS Med 2(8): e124. doi:10.1371/journal.pmed.0020124 (2005). Quickly found on-line at: journals.plos.org/plosmedicine/article?id=10.1371/journal.pmed.0020124.

2 Steve Donelan, my friend, cites the following sources for his Prologue:
http://www.photius.com/rankings/healthranks.html
Source: WHO World Health Report - See also Spreadsheet Details (731kb)

The World Health Organization's ranking of the world's health systems was last produced in 2000, and the WHO no longer produces such a ranking table, because of the complexity of the task.

Steve Donelan's work can be seen at: www.wildernessemergencycare.com. Steve's published book, *Wilderness Emergency Care*, (updated 2012) can be found on his website. The 2005 version can be found on: www.Amazon.com.

3 On mazes and labyrinths: I have thought of the institutional morass that I and others deal with after trauma—including after accidents and illnesses—as both a maze and a labyrinth, though these are somewhat different in form. Some traumas are experienced more as a maze, and others more as a labyrinth. A *maze* is a complex branching—multicursal— puzzle that includes choices of path and direction; it may have multiple entrances, exits, and dead ends. A *labyrinth* is unicursal and has only a single, non-branching path that leads to the center and then back out the same way, so there is one entry/exit point.

Monetary greed of corporations has created a situation in which the U.S. healthcare system now has a monster to contend with, like the minotaur in the labyrinth in Crete. The minotaur had the body of a man with the head of a bull, hence the term "bull-headed." The labyrinth had a complicated winding path to the center, with the minotaur a mortal threat to all that dared enter, until he was finally killed. Interesting that Wall Street calls a stock market with rising values a "bull market," though presumably because a bull thrusts its horns up into the air as it attacks opponents.

4 For Integrative Medicine: see Notes as for Chapter 13.

5 My excellent insurance agency is: Dawn Fairbanks Insurance Services, Inc. at: 510-339-1483 or www.fairbanks-ins.com. All agents that I have spoken with there are excellent, and my personal agent there is Nicole Slovinec.

6 My excellent tax attorney is: Douglas G. Murken, JD, 2135 Lombard St., San Francisco, CA 94123. Doug is an attorney specializing in taxation, business transactions, and real estate transactions. He can be reached at 415-749-5900 or www.smdjtlaw.com.

7 Helen Hempel, JD: same Note as for Chapter 9.

Chapter 20: Facing The Mountain

1 Jean Mayer arrived in Taos Ski Valley in 1957. There he developed the Ernie Blake Ski School, known for its unique and excellent instruction that combines the best techniques of modern skiing, and he is still the Technical Director in Taos and instructor of the top level ski class. Jean

began the Hotel St. Bernard in 1958, at the base of the ski runs, and still operates his hotel and serves the delicious French meals for this European style ski experience. See: www.stbernardtaos.com for more information or call 575-776-2251. See also: www.skitaos.org.

2 Ed Pettit, PhD, is my eldest brother, a now retired math and computer science professor; we were the first persons in my family to ski.

3 Dave Pettit: same Note as for Chapter 2.

4 International Summer Camp Montana was founded in 1961 by Rudy Studer. Philippe Studer, Rudy's and Erica's son, now carries on the philosophy of his parents, with the help of relatives and staff: providing recreational education to young people, knowing they will benefit through sports and international friendship. See more at: www.campmontana.ch, or call +41-27-486-8686.

5 Nicole, my daughter: same Note as for Chapter 17.

6 Canadian Mountain Holidays (CMH) is the oldest and largest heli-skiing company in the world. Hans Gmoser, a mountain guide from Austria who immigrated to Canada in 1951, conceived the idea of using helicopters to ski in wilderness terrain and then began this unique sport in 1965 in the Bugaboos. Now there are 12 lodges with ski terrain in the wilderness that are open in the winter for heli-skiing. The Monashees Lodge is one of these, with skiing in the Monashees Mountain Range, lying mostly in British Columbia, Canada; this area is best known for its steep and deep skiing among trees (one run there is named "Steep and Deep" and another is named "Elevator;" these have been featured in Warren Miller movies). More information about CMH on their website: www.canadianmountainholidays.com or by phone: 1-800-661-0252.

7 The Haute Route is the name given to a route undertaken on foot or by ski touring between Chamonix in France and Zermatt in Switzerland. See www.haute-route.com.

8 Mt. Kongur: see first Note for Chapter 5.

9 Roger Laurilla, ski and mountain guide as well as photographer extraordinaire, was the manager of the Monashees Lodge and now (2015) in the winter is working at Battle Abbey, remote wilderness lodge (see: www.battleabbey.ca), and rarely in the Monashees. Roger directs his own company; see: www.realandwildadventures.com.

10 Joan Provencher; same Note as for Chapter 4.

Chapter 21: Resetting the Course

1 CalOSHA is the California Division of Occupational Safety and Health. It is charged with inspecting chairlifts twice a year to make certain they meet structural safety standards. They do little to ensure the safety of lift operators and attendants, however, and mandated operations are rarely observed, according to Dick Penniman. CalOSHA does not have anything to do with slopes and trails. Website: www.dir.ca.gov/dosh.

2 California Ski and Snowboard Safety Organization (CSSSO) was formed in 2007. California is the second biggest ski state in the nation, just behind Colorado. Unlike many states, California has no safety statute, and the ski industry has no uniform safety code. Pressure has resulted in ski resorts providing a Family Safety Report Card. This report card can be seen on the website below, and so far it is not good: the overall grade for most resorts averages C, only two average B, seven average D, and one averages F, as of 2015. I urge you to check out the resort's report card before you plan a ski vacation or buy a season pass. Clearly below a C grade is not acceptable. It will be good if the grades for safety improve with consumer pressure. See information at: www.calskisafety.org; email at: info@calskisafety.org. (January 2016: the Family Safety Report Card on the CSSSO website and the CSSSO are now linked to the SnowSport Safety Foundation, also on the website below.)

3 Dick Penniman is the Chief Research Officer for SnowSport Safety Foundation, established in 2008. The foundation's address is: 1484 Page St., San Francisco, CA 94117; website at: www.snowsportsafetyfoundation.org, or phone: 415-839-6716. Dan Gregorie founded and is President of the SnowSport Safety Foundation.

4 Ibid.

5 Ibid.

6 Ron Wecht, JD, my attorney, is retired and no longer practicing law. Ron was a partner at the Walkup Law Firm in San Francisco, which provides excellent personal injury representation. Website for the firm is: www.walkuplawoffice.com, and phone: 415-981-7210. (January 2016).

7 The physiatrist who examined me in preparation for being an expert witness for my jury trial was Deborah Doherty, MD, at Kentfield Hospital in Kentfield, CA, Marin County. Dr. Doherty completed a Physical Medicine and Rehabilitation Residency at Stanford University Medical Center. She has been the Medical Director of the Brain Injury Rehabilitation Program at Kentfield Hospital since 1985 and is the Chief Medical Officer for CareMeridian, which provides subacute resider tial services to brain

injured individuals. Information and contact via Dr. Doherty's work phone: 415-485-3509.

8 Nicole Petiet, my daughter: same Note as for Chapter 17.

Chapter 22: Mystery and Miracles

1 Anita Barrows and Joanna Macy, trans and eds., *In Praise of Mortality: Selections from Rainer Maria Rilke's Duino Elegies and Sonnets to Orpheus* (New York: Riverhead Books, Penguin, 2005), 115.

2 Albert Einstein, *Living Philosophies: A Series of Intimate Credos* (New York: Simon & Schuster, Inc., 1931), I.

3 Jim Pettit, PhD: same Note as for Chapter 2.

4 Toby Rowland-Jones: same Note as for Chapter 1.

5 Greg Hawthorne and family can be found via their magnificent art gallery on Highway One in Big Sur, CA: Hawthorne Gallery – Big Sur; phone 831-667-3200; see: www.hawthornegallery.com.

6 Dixie Pierson, PhD, remarkable woman and friend, was a bat research scientist living in Berkeley, CA. She is now deceased.

7 Margaret Allen, PhD: same Note as for Preface.

8 A shamanic view of Power Animal is: the spirit of an animal that comes to you to lend wisdom and power for your life and health. Native Americans, the people of Mother Earth, have traditionally been drawn to real animals as a means of seeking wisdom and messages from the Great Spirit. Messages exist in all of nature but are thought to be most predominant in the animal clan. Each animal has certain qualities for teaching us.

9 Eagle represents: spirit vision, strength, courage, swiftness, keen sight, wisdom, and healing.

10 Maggie Phillips, PhD, is a licensed psychologist who has a private practice in Oakland, CA. She is also an expert in clinical hypnosis, teaches internationally, and has published a number of books and CDs, with foci including healing pain and the mind-body connection (see www.amazon.com for her Author Page and items available). For more information see: www.maggiephillipsphd.com or call 510-655-3843.

11 I learned about vision/wilderness fasts with Steven Foster and Meredith Little, then with Joan Halifax:

Meredith Little runs the School of Lost Borders, which she founded and developed with her husband Steven Foster (deceased in 2003). The School of Lost Borders is based in CA, where vision fast and rites of passage have been taught and offered for 35 years. Steven and Meredith wrote several books, including: *The Book of the Vision Quest* (1980), which is still available in a revised edition. Many papers and audio resources are available on their website. For more information see: www.schooloflostborders.org or call 760-938-3333.

Roshi Joan Halifax is a Buddhist teacher, Zen Priest, and anthropologist who founded the Upaya Institute and Zen Center in Santa Fe, New Mexico in 1990. Joan teaches, has written many books and has a Joan Halifax Author Page on www.amazon.com. Many other written resources are available on the Upaya website. See: www.upaya.org or call 505-986-8518.

12 A number of books have been written about the power of prayer. Books by leading Integrative Medicine practitioners (see Notes in Chapter 13) include:

Larry Dossey, MD, *The Power of Prayer and the Practice of Medicine* (New York: Harper Collins Pub, 1993).

Larry Dossey, MD, *Prayer is Good Medicine: How to Reap the Healing Benefits of Prayer* (San Francisco: Harper, 1996).

Jon Kabat-Zin, et al., *The Power of Meditation and Prayer* (Santa Rosa, CA: New Dimentions Radio, 1997).

13 Jay Morgan, MD: same Note as for Chapter 1.

14 Steven Kennedy, MD, was part of the Trauma Team at Washoe: same Note as for Chapter 1.

15 Martyn ___: same Note as for Chapter 11.

16 Hotel St. Bernard: same Note as for Chapter 20.

17 Wilmer Eye Institute at Johns Hopkins, 600 N. Wolfe St., Baltimore, MD 21287; www.hopkinsmedicine.org/wilmer/; or call 410-955-5080.

18 Allen Putterman, MD, 111 N. Wabash Ave., Suite 1722, Chicago, IL 60602; email: drputterman@gmail.com; or call 312-372-2256.

19 Stuart R. Seiff, MD, FACS: same Note as for Chapter 11. Dr. Seiff has offices in San Francisco and San Mateo. Call 415-923-3007. (See Chapter 11 for my eye healing saga, during which I intuitively sought and benefitted from Integrative Medicine; also see Notes for Chapter 13.)

20 Marcia Black, PhD: same Note as for Chapter 16.

21 Peter Levine, PhD: same Note as for Chapter 16.

22 Esalen Institute: same Note as for Chapter 16.

23 Ariel Giarretto, LMFT: same Note as for Chapter 17.

24 Eye surgeries are described in Chapter 11.

25 Cathy Adachi, RPT: same Note as for Chapter 11.

26 Kathy Kain, MA: same Note as for Chapter 11.

27 Steve Hoskinson, MA, is a senior faculty member with the Somatic Experiencing Trauma Institute™ and can be seen on the SETI website: www.traumahealing.org. Steve lives in Encinitas, CA and has a private practice there; call 760-634-3691. Steve teaches internationally and has his own website at: www.hoskinsonconsulting.org/.

28 "All shall be well" is from Julian of Norwich, an English woman from the 14th century who is venerated as an important Christian mystic. See:

Julian of Norwich, *Revelations of Divine Love* (14th century, trans. Father John-Julian (Brewster, MA: Parclete, 2011), 64.

Also found at: https://www.christianhistoryinstitute.org/incontext/article/julian/ in which she is quoted as saying: "… all shall be well, and all manner of thing shall be well."

29 Chris Carter, *Science and the Near-Death Experience: How Consciousness Survives Death* (Rochester, VT: Inner Traditions, 2010). Carter provides massive empirical evidence about the existence of the soul.

Chapter 23: Acceptance

1 The Serenity Prayer is the common name for a prayer authored by the American theologian Reinhold Niebuhr (1892–1971). It has been adopted by Alcoholics Anonymous and other twelve-step programs.

2 Sandi John, friend and colleague since we worked together in an inpatient alcohol and drug treatment program in Berkeley, CA, 1975-78, has since received many further degrees and work experiences: MDiv, MSN, PMHCNS, MFT, and spiritual direction. Sandi currently lives and works in Chico, CA. See photo and write up about Rev. Sandi John by googling Sandi John, MFT, Chico, CA, and then click the Psychology Today web link. Call her at 530-418-8903 or email at: revsandijohn@gmail.com.

3 Gerry Adamson is now retired and enjoying that freedom.

4 Jay Morgan, MD: same Note as for Chapter 1.

5 Deepak Chopra, MD, is an endocrinologist, practitioner of Aruyveda—an ancient healing tradition from India—and a gifted author and speaker. His many books focus on healing, wholeness, and the holy; these can be found at www.amazon.com. The relevant book for this chapter is:

Deepak Chopra, *Reinventing the Body, Resurrecting the Soul: How to Create a New You* (New York: Harmony Books, 2009).

I heard Deepak talk about the "holiness of healing" at the First Congregational Church in Berkeley, CA, March 3, 2008.

6 Integrative Medicine: same Notes as for Chapter 13.

Chapter 24: Gratitude

1 Henri J.M. Nouwen, *The Return of the Prodigal Son: A Story of Homecoming* (New York: Doubleday Pub., 1992), 86.

Henri Nouwen, late Catholic priest, psychologist, and devotional writer, knew that gratitude is a choice.

2 This quote that became a French Proverb is attributed to Jean Massieu, 1772-1846, a pioneering deaf educator (Google his name at: wikipedia.org, or google the proverb itself; August, 2015).

This French Proverb is quoted in the excellent book on gratitude:

Robert Emmons, *Thanks!: How the New Science of Gratitude Can Make You Happier* (New York: Houghton Mifflin Co., 2007), 89.

Dr. Emmons is a psychologist at the University of California at Davis who has studied gratitude for 14 years. Google: emmons lab uc davis, for more detailed information about his articles and books. Also see his easy to read article:

http://greatergood.berkeley.edu/article/item/why_gratitude_is_good.

3 John White, PhD, is a friend and colleague who has a private practice in Fremont and in Oakland, CA; call 510-768-8220, or email at: dr.johnrwhite@gmail.com. See further contact information, photo, and write up about him by googling John R. White, PhD, Oakland, CA, and then click the Psychology Today web link.

4 Toby Rowland-Jones: same Note as for Chapter 1.

5 Gratitude is a word that comes from the Latin word "gratia" which means grace, graciousness, gratefulness. Gratitude is strongly and consistently associated with: greater happiness, sense of well-being, enthusiasm, and optimism; greater health—such as exercising more, having fewer medical visits, a stronger immune system plus greater energy and alertness; determination and bouncing back more quickly from adversity; feeling free to express concerns if gratitude is also being expressed, and this combination leads to stronger social relationships; being more likely to help others, having greater progress toward achieving personal goals as well as more motivation to work when an employer expresses gratitude.

Suggestions for cultivating gratitude include: write thank-you notes; in addition to direct expressions of thankfulness, also thank people mentally; keep a gratitude journal; count your blessings; pray; and meditate.

Robert A. Emmons, *Gratitude Works!: A 21-Day Program for Creating Emotional Prosperity* (San Francisco, CA: Jossey-Bass, 2013).

See R.A. Emmons et al, "In Praise of Gratitude," *Harvard Mental*

Health Letter, November 1, 2011; available at: http://www.health.harvard.edu/newsletter_article/in-praise-of-gratitude .

There are numerous excellent books and articles about the benefits of gratitude and the practice of gratitude, in addition to Emmons above. Some of these are:

Angeles Arrien, *Living in Gratitude: A Journey that Will Change your Life* (Boulder, CO: Sounds True, Inc., 2011).

Sarah Ban Breathnach, *The Simple Abundance Journal of Gratitude* (New York: Warner Books, 1996).

R.A. Emmons, et al, "Counting Blessings Versus Burdens: An Experiential Investigation of Gratitude and Subjective Well-Being in Daily Life," *Journal of Personality and Social Psychology* Vol.84, No.2 (Feb. 2003), 377-89.

R.A. Emmons and Michael E. McCullough, *The Psychology of Gratitude* (New York: Oxford Univ. Press, 2004).

G.M. Grant, et al, "A Little Thanks Goes a Long Way: Explaining Why Gratitude Expressions Motivate Prosocial Behavior," *Journal of Personality and Social Psychology* Vol.98, No.6 (June 2010), 946-55.

N.M. Lanert, et al, "Expressing Gratitude to a Partner Leads to More Relationship Maintenance Behavior," *Emotion* Vol.11, No.1 (Feb. 2011), 52-60.

R.A. Sansone, et al, "Gratitude and Well Being: The Benefits of Appreciation," *Psychiatry* Vol.7, No.11 (Nov. 2010), 18-22.

Brother David Steindl-Rast, *Gratefulness, the Heart of Prayer: An Approach to Life in Fullness* (Mahwah, N.J.: Paulist Press, 1984).

Online resources include:

Marelisa Fabrega, "How Gratitude Can Change Your Life," see: http://www.thechangeblog.com/gratitude/.

www.greatergood.berkeley.edu has many articles, videos, and summaries on gratitude. Type "gratitude" in the search area on the website.

www.gratefulness.org is Brother David Steindl-Rast's informative, helpful, and supportive website about gratefulness. He offers via this website free subscription to a "Word for the Day" for contemplation and meditation.

Acknowledgements

I am indebted to Toby Rowland-Jones and Dr. Jay Morgan for saving my life. Words cannot express my gratefulness for your availability, skill, and hard work on my behalf.

Teachers, healers, and my own clients have oriented me toward the journey back to engaged life after trauma. Family and friends have supported and sustained me with help, love, feedback, and humor. For all of you, I am deeply grateful.

My daughter Nicole and friend Susan Phillips have provided the precious sustenance of near daily contact, as did frequent contact with friends Margaret Allen and Ayala Pines as well as my parents when they were alive. I particularly acknowledge my mother, Ann Johnson, who always believed in me and encouraged me to spread my wings. My siblings have provided a backdrop of love and availability, and I honor you: Ed, Jim, and Dave Pettit; Father Justin Sinaites, Cecilia Grossman, and Kenneth Hicks when he was alive. My large extended family has provided a palpable grounding during my adventures, traumas, and the writing of this book. Mima Baird and Sandi John have enriched my life with our women's group since January1979 as well as with our special pilgrimages together, generously offering help in countless ways, and thankfully Susan Phillips has been in our group since 1990; Maryann Aberg, Heide Parreno, and Mary Spence were with us for portions of our years together—all are special soul sisters.

Thank you Phil Cousineau for your writing and inspiration, including *Stoking the Creative Fires*.... I was thinking of writing my book while reading your book. The result was that I put your book down, picked up a note pad, began and continued writing *The Day I Died.*

This book has greatly benefitted from careful reading, editing, and feedback from Steve Donelan, Susan Phillips, Dave Pettit, and Ed Pettit. Thank you, Steve, for your tireless editing and support as my book was formed. Thank you, Susan, for your wise counsel during my whole writing ordeal and for helping me learn to navigate digital life. Thank you, Dave, for your poetic sensibility as we brainstormed and developed chapter titles while enjoying a ski vacation. Thank you, Steve, Dave, and Ed, for reading every word. Others have read portions of the many iterations as this book was formed, and your advice helped shape it: Mima Baird, Marcia Black, Lois Inman Engle, Chuck and Sandi John, Joel Kramer, Jean Mayer, Alexander Nemeth, Dick Penniman, Ayala Pines, Kathryn Ridall, Carol Sazama Robbins, Mary and Roger Spence, Ron Spinka, Brenda Townes, Ron Wecht, Jeanne Wetzel-Chinn, and John White.

A special thank you to Ayala Pines, who tirelessly encouraged me in writing this book and also wrote the Foreword before her untimely death. Ayala provided the model, experience, and feedback of a skilled psychologist author during our long friendship and Esalen "sister weeks," especially helped me remember and clarify my voice as she encouraged me to challenge healthcare providers toward excellence.

Another special thank you to those who graciously wrote prologues for chapters of this book: Mima Baird, Marcia Black, Craig, Steve Donelan, Sandi John, Jean Mayer, Dick Penniman, Nicole Petiet, Jim Pettit, Susan Phillips, Toby Rowland-Jones, Brenda Townes, and John White. Thank you, Gerry Adamson and your family, for generously sharing your powerful experiences of different types of acceptance along your healing journeys. All of you who helped form this book have enriched my words as well as my life in unique and blessed ways.

It is said that "it takes a village" to raise a child. In my experience, it also took a village to support me along the journey back to full life after severe trauma. My heart is full of gratitude for the loving support of many persons: family, friends, and healers. The plethora of acts of kindness and generosity feel nearly endless. Nicole, thank you for the joy and love we have shared, for giving me the complex and challenging lessons of parenthood, for being the remarkable woman you are and my precious daughter. Margaret Allen arrived in Reno shortly after my brain surgery, helped my clients and psychology practice in Berkeley cope with the trauma of my accident, and always shared with deep, multifaceted attunement as a cherished friend. Margaret Allen and Dixie Pierson also did shamanic journeys to support my living as soon as they heard about my accident; I miss you both. Other friends and family around the world prayed, chanted, visualized, meditated, and lit candles for my healing.

Craig saw me as I had been before my accident—while many others reacted to me with fear—and this was crucial for reclaiming what somatic therapists call my embodied *felt sense*; I appreciate your many acts of love, including talking with doctors when I could not, listening to my venting when I could talk, your touch, humor, and keen intelligence as well as multiple acts of help and fun at home and the cabin. Donna Gilio and her family provided housing and transport for Nicole to visit me while I was in the hospital in Reno; thank you and Mary Berge for being my spiritual ski buddies. Jerry, thank you for coming to Reno to help and for driving Nicole back to Berkeley. Brothers Jim and Dave Pettit, your showing up in Reno to be with me when you thought I might die was profound; Dave and Kelley, thank you also for coming to stay with me in Berkeley as you helped with my medical appointments, Nicole, and our home shortly after I was released from the rehabilitation hospital. Thank you Dorothy and Max Pettit, two of my now deceased parents, for also coming to Berkeley to help after my accident, and thank you Nicole's father for coming to help her. Thank you Maryann Aberg for your emotional support as you also provided important paperwork for my financial survival shortly after I returned home.

Susan Phillips, you filled me with astonishment and gratitude as you made time available to drive me to many medical appointments and helped me laugh at absurdities; then you encouraged and taught me as I wrote this book. Thank you Lois Inman Engle for providing crucial support for Nicole and for me, always, including bringing Nicole to the rehabilitation hospital with delicious food for me, as well as helping me craft crucial words in this book. Marilee Stark, along with your daughters Lily and Hana, thank you for providing essential support and housing for Nicole while I was still in the rehabilitation hospital. Marlene and Hilary Sanders, thank you for also providing critical support for Nicole immediately after my accident and for later helping Nicole visit and bring special food to me in the rehabilitation hospital. Thank you Joan Provencher for your distinct friendship and for helping my aching body with your skilled daily massages—an all-important gift while I was in rehabilitation (and for many years). Mima Baird, thank you for helping Nicole in vital ways: you generously took Nicole to trauma treatment appointments and also played and listened with Nicole in profound ways; you have always provided steady, deep, quiet, loving support for me; journeying with you for so many years has blessed my life immensely.

Dana McMullen, thank you for helping my clients and psychology practice, also for orchestrating a celebration of my return to work with a circle of women friends and colleagues. A special group of women worked together to help my psychology practice and clients survive my unexpected absence: Margaret Allen, Mima Baird, Lila Coulter, Deeahna Lorenz, Dana McMullen, Kathryn Ridall, Mary Spence, and Marilee Stark.

Thank you Kathryn Ridall for driving me to many medical

appointments and for your poetic sensibility in forming important and pithy words for this book, including the title. Thank you Brenda Townes for helping me understand what happened in the rehabilitation hospital as you provided your strong, wise, and loving support. Friends from important groups reached out to support me: my Tahoe ski buddies, especially Donna Gilio, Maggie Hakansson, Mary Berge, Diane Lott, and Carla Shnier; my heli-ski buddies, especially Richard Barrett, Andy Littman, and guide Roger Laurilla; Jean Mayer and the St. Bernard Hotel staff in Taos Ski Valley, New Mexico, as well as ski friendships formed there, including Martyn who helped me get excellent eye surgery in San Francisco. Thank you Marcia Black for your friendship and for helping me find SE™; this helped with Nicole's healing and later with mine as well as opened the door to expanding and integrating my professional practice as a nurse and psychologist. Thank you Dora Maltz for reaching out and supporting me with love from Paris as well as when we finally did get to Paris. I also have been blessed by other dear friends who visited and supported me in the hospital and afterward, including Jennifer Palangio and Joel Kramer, Ernie Bryant and Mary Cunningham, Barry Fields, Bill Koch, Mary Krentz, Marty Freedman, and Ron Spinka. Dear soul friends from pre-Berkeley days also reached out across the miles with loving support: Ursula Frieman, Irene Goldbeck, Carol Sazama Robbins, Chris Senn, and Carol Traut.

Thank you to photographers James Garrahan for your kind, flexible, and tuned in ways as well as your tremendous skill in portrait photography and Roger Laurilla for your expertise in outdoor, mountain, and athletic photography as well as your generous skill as mountain guide and resort manager. Thank you Badar Aslam of Piedmont Copy and Printing (Oakland, CA, 510-655-3030) for your skilled, detailed, and kind work in digitalizing my old personal photos for this book. Thank you John White for your spiritual and photographic sensibilities that improved this book and enrich my life.

I want to recognize and affirm the many excellent helpers and expert professionals that I met during my healing journey. Brian Clark helped me on the ski slope immediately after my accident, alongside Toby Rowland-Jones and other ski team supporters. The ski patrol and slopeside medical clinic got me safely readied for the helicopter flight to the hospital. Dr. Steven Kennedy expertly managed my arrival and care in the emergency room as I was prepared for surgery. Dr. Jay Morgan provided healing neurosurgery and then oversaw my care in the trauma ICU. A number of nurses, physical therapists, and one physician in the rehabilitation hospital were kind and helpful. Dr. Richard Litwin was the first ophthalmologist I saw outside a hospital; thank you for helping me understand my hospital experience as well as understand the need to slowly navigate my eye-healing journey. Other expert ophthalmologists who helped my eye healing were Dr. Richard Imes and accomplished surgeons Dr. Stuart Seiff, Dr. Creig Hoyt, and Dr. Douglas Fredrick. Alternative healers who helped my eye healing were Greg Schelkun and Meir Schneider as well as my acupuncturist Lynn Segura, craniosacral therapists Cathy Adachi and Katrina Auer, and Somatic Experiencing® therapists Ariel Giaretto and Kathy Kain. A special thank you to internal medicine Dr. Priya Yerasi who expertly oversaw my post-hospital medical care, along with neurologist Dr. Irene Pech. Rehab Without Walls oversaw my rehab needs after discharge from the Bay Area hospital for inpatient rehabilitation, provided creative physical therapists and rehabilitation psychotherapist-neuropsychologist Dr. Carrie Thaler who skillfully helped me navigate returning to work. Chiropractors Dr. Scott Phillips and Dr. David Doan helped me heal from a frozen shoulder and helped my body relax more fully. Thank you Dr. David Chan for helping to keep my body in one properly aligned piece as I resumed my athletic endeavors. Dr. Peter Levine, founder of Somatic Experiencing®, trained the skilled somatic healers that Nicole and I saw: Ariel Giarretto, Julia Gombos, and Kathy Kain. Thank you each, Ariel, Julia, and Kathy, for your kindness and your talented expertise, and thank you Ariel, Kathy, Steve Hoskinson, and Peter for your accomplished teaching: the SE™ treatment approach has changed my professional understanding and work. Behavioral pediatrician Dr. Joan Lovett did multifaceted and helpful EMDR sessions with Nicole shortly after I got out of the rehabilitation hospital. Thank you Dr. Francine Shapiro for developing EMDR and teaching it to me in the late 1980s.

Ski safety expert Dick Penniman generously helped me understand what went awry in that ski race and referred me to attorney Ron Wecht who skillfully and courageously navigated my legal efforts regarding ski race safety. Attorney Helen Hempel kindly helped me navigate the legal process for parents at the end of their lives.

Dr. Kenneth Cooper deserves special recognition for his role as The Father of Aerobics, for his research that began clarifying the health value of aerobic exercise in the late 1960s. Following Dr. Cooper's suggestions helped provide me with adequate physical foundation to survive the trauma of my accident.

About the Author

Carole Petiet, PhD, SEP, RN, lives and works in Berkeley, California. She has a private practice as a clinical psychologist and hands-on somatic practitioner (SE™). She also works in supervision and consultation with other professionals. Carole has been working as a helping professional for more than 40 years and is passionate about living and loving fully. She is a family woman, athlete, lover of music and the arts, and a world traveler.

Visit her website at: www.carolepetietphd.com

CPSIA information can be obtained
at www.ICGtesting.com
Printed in the USA
FSOW02n0032190117
29802FS